Praise and Endorsements for *With Unwashed Hands: A True Story*

As a foreign missionary, I kept hearing of Darrell and Joanie Bolton and how God had been using them throughout the Asian countries helping and encouraging both the missionaries and the national pastors. Although I have never met them in person, I feel I have become better acquainted with them through *With Unwashed Hands*. I have read the book twice, each time in a single sitting. The first time I was enthralled by the story of what they endured. The second time I read it more closely, looking for how God was working and preparing them for even greater things in the future. God has truly refined the Boltons, and they "have come forth as gold." *With Unwashed Hands* is a story of courage and of the amazing grace of a loving God.

– Dr. Charlie Vest, Founder
Asian World Baptist Ministries

Here is a true and intriguing story of one couple's journey of faith in God in the midst of life-threatening obstacles. What should have been a place to spare lives became a place that almost cost them the husband's life. Read with fascination their emotional faith-building experience.

– Dr. Mike Mutchler, Pastor
Grand View Baptist Church, Beavercreek, Oregon

This is a story of faith, miracles, and love. It proves the point that what man means for evil, God can use for good. Break out your box of tissues, prepare to have your heart wrenched out, and your soul inspired.

– Sandra Stiles, *Author*
Steps to Courage

The harrowing story of Darrell and Joanie Bolton during their 2011 missions trip reminded me of Joseph, who said this about those who had tried to harm him: *"But as for you, ye thought evil against me; but God meant it unto good, to bring to pass, as it is this day, to save much people alive"* (Genesis 50:20).

With Unwashed Hands is a tribute to God's divine protection, proving again and again that God is worthy of our trust. There is absolutely no denying that God turned a trial to triumph. Once you start reading, you won't stop until you get to the end of this miraculous story.

– Francie Taylor, *Editor in Chief*
Keep the Heart

From the cover to the last word, this book not only appealed to my senses as an avid reader, it enhanced my faith as I read of the journey of two people who desired nothing more than to spread the Gospel and became physically attacked by the evil forces of this world.

Reading about the reality of the crisis the Boltons endured, coupled with fear of the unknown, you stand amazed at their childlike faith in the all-encompassing power of our Savior and Father in heaven!

Their story is riveting, and the writer has the incredible talent of making you feel every emotion they experienced with each incredible, surreal event that took place. This book is a "must-read," and I can visualize a movie in the making!

– Christine Z. DeWitte, *Author*
When I Fall, Please Grab My Hand

The humor, wit, poignancy, and compassion made this book an exceptional read! This book is a great example of how God, with His mighty hand, carries us through dark days.

– N. A. Scott, MA, BA, *Christian educator*

This book tells the true story of the harrowing experience of the Boltons during a mission trip to a third-world country. This trip nearly cost Darrell his life—not because of any law being broken or any custom being defiled; rather, it was because of a prejudicial doctor who intentionally neglected every known medical hygiene standard during a major surgery. However, that is not the only lesson in this book. It is a true and inspiring story of triumph as well. The grace of God—a grace that the Boltons had to rely on—is woven into the fabric of the pages like a fine tapestry.

This book is a must-read, and I highly recommend it for everyone!

– Pastor W. Delton Kilpatrick
South Middleburg Baptist Church
Middleburg, Florida

Darrell Bolton was on a mission trip when he needed medical attention immediately. When he was taken to the doctor, a man that you need to be able to trust with your life, things only got worse. Darrell and his wife would soon discover the doctor's secret motive was to put him in the morgue—simply because of a military career that had long been over. The writing is superb. It's easy, breezy, and yet heavy with meaning and emotions. It will be in your mind for weeks after.

This book is heartfelt, suspenseful, tragic, and hopeful all at the same time. Lessons the couple learned will hit home and really stick, and that's the best type of reading there is.

– Samantha Coville
Sammy the Bookworm, Finding the Gems

As I follow the ministry of retired Air Force officer Darrell Bolton and his wife Joanie, the words of the apostle Paul found in II Corinthians 11:26 and 27 reverberate loudly in my mind: *"In journeyings often, in perils of waters, in perils of robbers, in perils by mine own countrymen, in perils by the heathen, in perils in the city, in perils in the wilderness, in perils in the sea, in perils among false brethren; In weariness and painfulness, in watchings often, in hunger and in thirst, in fastings often, in cold and nakedness."*

Shadowing the spirit of the great missionaries of old—David Livingstone in Africa, Adoniram Judson in Burma, or Hudson Taylor in China, these modern-day servants of God, Darrell and Joanie Bolton, continue to live a sacrificial life filled with testings, trials, and sufferings. Their goal is to see a great harvest of souls reaped for the Lord Jesus Christ to the glory of God.

Thank you, Darrell and Joanie Bolton, for your willingness to remain faithful in the face of adversity.

– Dr. Dennis Higgins, *Pastor*
Harbor Baptist Church
Hainesport, New Jersey

One of the blessings in my field of work is getting to know giants of the faith like Darrell and Joanie Bolton. As I worked with Joanie on this manuscript, my heart was blessed numerous times through emails and telephone calls. The Boltons have a heart for the work of Christ. *With Unwashed Hands* is a book to read many times—not just once.

– Linda Stubblefield, Editor
Affordable Christian Editing

I have personally known the Boltons for many years. I remember Brother Bolton's coming on missionary trips as a team member to South East Asia, then I watched God begin to birth a ministry in their heart and to expand their coast to many countries around the world.

In this well-written book, you will be challenged and inspired to walk closer to God. You will travel with the Boltons on their journey of faith to follow God in obedience to His will for their lives. This book is a must-read for every believer. It is a life changer!

– Dr. Mike Wells, Pastor
Parkside Baptist Church
Mesquite, Texas

This is a remarkable story of unbelievable hardships, shocking adversity, and painful emotions, but it is countered by abundant mercy, miraculous grace, and divine intervention. This compelling adventure is, within itself, more than enough to arrest the attention of our hearts, it will enhance your faith and strengthen your walk with God.

– Eddie R. Galyean
Missionary to the Philippines

ISBN: 979-8-9860186-0-7
Yellow Bird Press, LLC
www.withunwashedhands.com

This book is a work of nonfiction. Some names have been changed, no characters have been invented, and no events have been fabricated. *Darrell and Joanie Bolton are both available for speaking engagements. To contact us via email: withunwashedhands@gmail.com*

To see more pictures and video taken during the trip, please visit our website: www.withunwashedhands.com

Proceeds from this book will be used on future mission trips.

INTERIOR FORMATTING
Linda Stubblefield, *Arrow Computer Services*

COVER DESIGN
Aaron McBride, *Radiance Graphic Design*

All Scripture in this book are from the King James Bible.

Printed and Bound in the United States

Dedication

THIS BOOK IS lovingly dedicated to the following very special people:

- The first is our Heavenly Father, the Great Physician. He was our "...stronghold in the day of trouble" (Nahum 1:7). He was also our Comforter in times of intense physical pain and deep heartache. He showered us with such amazing grace and mercy; He even protected us from recognizing troubling events at the time they actually occurred.

- The second person is our physician's assistant (PA) Mary Jo Sutherland. Because of her compassionate care for our family, and for me personally, she was instrumental in indirectly saving my husband's life.

- The last dedication is to the best prayer warriors we know. We are humbled and thankful for the untold prayers said on our behalf. I believe that my husband was the most prayed-for person on planet Earth during our specific trying days. Many have shared that because their night was our day (we were on the other side of the world when these events unfolded), they would get up in the middle of the night to pray and check for updates on their computers. With our situations changing dramatically by the day, and often by the hour, they were able to pray specifically for our needs.

To those that so unselfishly chose to forego sleep on our behalf, I offer you my heartfelt thanks.

In the fall of 2012, Darrell and Joanie Bolton visited us in the Philippines. We had met Brother Darrell on previous mission trips, but this was our first time to meet Joanie. One night as they ate supper with us, they told us the gripping story of *With Unwashed Hands.* Over the next few months we prayed for them as they worked on publishing this story, which you now hold in your hands. May God greatly use and bless it to HIS honor and glory!

– Rick & Becky Martin
Missionaries to the Philippines

Acknowledgments

I wish to thank my husband, Darrell, who gave me the freedom to write until 2:00 a.m. (and often later) most evenings—for over a year. As the book came closer to completion, he took over some cooking and dishwashing duties to allow me the extra time needed at the computer. Darrell, my simple written "acknowledgment" could never express what your help and sacrifice of our time together has meant to make this book possible. Your unexpected offer to help edit absolutely thrilled me. Since we lived this trial together, you understood what my heart longed to share. I am thankful for all your help, and I am deeply thankful that I still have you.

To Julie Brown, one of the busiest ladies I know. With a full-time job, homeschooling your children, and your involvement in ministry, your generous offer to edit my book completely stunned me. Your thorough work, despite your busy schedule, means so much! Your editing insights and knowledge were instrumental to my book being a success. Thank you!

Becky Driskell, my dear friend of 30 years! I have cherished our many phone calls which allowed me to express the intimate details of our experiences to accurately tell our story. Your amazing creativity and writing skills are invaluable. Thank you, precious friend!

To Beth Higgins and Elaine Snyder, you both offered invaluable insights of my early drafts, and as Becky put it, changed my book, "from diary to manuscript." I am extremely thankful you were candid enough to make the comments you have, which helped point me to a more serious writing style. Thank you!

Thank you, Aaron McBride, of Radiance Graphic Design, for the amazing book cover! You were beyond patient to allow me to convey what was pictured in my mind. In doing so, we have a stunning final product. I love my book cover, thank you so much!

To Linda Stubblefield, thank you for the wonderful job you did on my book layout, I love it! I would like to also thank you for the book cover suggestions, they were perfect!

To Chrissy Dewitte, thank you for the long phone calls where you selflessly took the time to share your experience and knowledge as a self-published author. Your encouragement has been priceless.

To Aja Ferrell, you're almost like a daughter to us. I want to thank you so much for your kind offer to edit our revised version of the book. You're such a blessing to us, and we love you very much!

Finally, to the best cheerleaders an author could ever have. I have received emails, phone calls, text messages and untold prayers during the entire writing process. There were times I wanted to toss aside this painful book-writing project, and you were there to encourage me along. You prayed us through the difficult events we experienced, and ultimately, through the writing of this book. Thank you, thank you!

Table of Contents

Preface 13
1 "You Want to Go to Eden Too?" 17
2 T-Minus Ten Days...and So Much to Do! 21
3 The Longest Night I Remember 25
4 Day 1—Extreme Highs, Extreme Lows 29
5 A Very Busy Day of Rest 35
6 An Arrogant First Impression 41
7 Treatment...and Mistreatment Begin 43
8 The Best Skype Call, Ever! 51
9 The First Surgery 55
10 The Worst Skype Call, Ever!. 59
11 The Hardest Call of My Life 67
12 A Spot of Tea 73
13 Heartbroken and So Far from Home 77
14 "Halfway to Heaven" 83
15 Surgery #2, On Demand! 91
16 ICU; Day One 97
17 ICU; Day Two 103
18 Old Man Shuffle 107

19 Memorial Service from Afar 101
20 Our Doctor Stoops to a New Low....111
21 Recovery Therapy 119
22 Just an Observation....123
23 Discharged—My New Favorite Word!....125
24 The Last Days in Eden 129
25 Arriving in Thailand....137
26 Another Hospital?! 141
27 And It's Back to the Operating Room!....147
28 A Twenty-First Century Good Samaritan....153
29 Darrell Released...Joanie Nearly Evicted!....157
30 Two Steps Forward, One Step Back 163
31 Amazing Last Days in Thailand 167
32 An Eventful Flight Home....175
33 "What? Another Hospital?!" 179
34 The Fourth and Final Surgery....183
35 Wounded, but Still in Action....189
36 We're Baaaack, Seven Years Later 193
37 Re-Reconstruction 199

One Final Thought....205

MVP Missions Ministry 207

Appendix....213

Comforting and Relevant Verses 215

Preface

As glamorous as it would be to begin by saying that writing a book was the fulfillment of a literary dream, I really cannot. If I did, it would shift this book over to the fiction category.

As we finally began to tell the graphic details and almost unbelievable experiences of our 2011 mission trip, nearly everyone who has heard them have insisted, "Please, please write a book!" The details of what we experienced show how God powerfully spared my husband's life, and at the same time, how He tenderly carried us through some perilous and heartbreaking times.

My name is Joanie Bolton, and my husband is Darrell Bolton, the founder and director of MVP Missions, the Missionary Volunteer Program. Darrell has been traveling on mission trips since 2007, and at this writing, has traveled to 32 different countries.

From the orphan who longs for a sign of affection to the lonely adult who's been shut away in a leper colony, Darrell loves to share the good news of God's unconditional love. After seeing thousands of his pictures and hearing about his amazing stories, he inspired me to go on a mission trip. I started traveling with him in 2010, and I have loved everything about these exciting trips.

After Darrell's retirement from serving 23 years in the United States Air Force, we would never have imagined that his military service could actually create opportunities for him to speak overseas. This is especially true in the Philippines, where the United States forces liberated the Filipino people from the Japanese attacks and subsequent occupation many years ago. Multiple times, because of his military background, the Filipino people would ask Darrell to preach even though other experienced pastors were standing by. It is amazing to see how God has enabled my once relatively shy husband to stand and boldly speak before very large crowds.

Darrell has the advantage of his military career, and interestingly, I found out that being blonde can have its own special perks on the mission field. On mission trips to Nevis in the West Indies, Africa, and Jamaica, some of the precious young girls could not resist reaching out to touch my long blonde hair.

Quite unexpectedly, Darrell's "advantage" became a life-threatening "disadvantage" when his Air Force career was revealed during a perilous medical situation while on a mission trip. Being unaware of political tensions between this country and the United States, my husband and I honestly answered the doctor's specific questions; we were American missionaries and Darrell was a retired Air Force officer. Upon that admission Darrell instantly became a double enemy to that doctor. He made this fact very clear by his anti-American comments, his body-language, and the horrible things he did and the important things he did not do for my husband, who was suddenly under his care.

We have learned you can never prepare yourself for the raw emotion and fear we suddenly faced—fear we were forced to keep bottled up within ourselves due to security concerns. Heads shaking, we would ask each other, "Is this really happening?!" With deafening silence, we would look around the room (usually a hospital or an emergency room), and we would know that these events were indeed "really happening."

For the safety and well-being of the missionaries still serving in the partially communist country where Darrell was treated (and mistreated), we have intentionally changed the name. For the duration of the book, I will refer to this country as "Eden," due to the amazing beauty there which specifically aided in both our physical and emotional recovery.

This book shares more than our sorrow and fear; it also reveals moments of grace, assurance, and many answers to prayer. There are technology miracles, sweet expressions of love, and even a little humor. Though some events were extremely difficult to endure, they were quickly followed by an abundance of mercy bestowed on us by both God and our fellow man.

Reliving the purposeful cruelty toward my husband and my great personal loss, it caused me to weep more while writing this book than when we were actually experiencing them. In order to tell this story accurately, Darrell and I had to finally share the painful details of the things we endured apart from each other—many months after they happened.

Perfectly timed, whenever I wanted to quit writing this book, I would cross paths with yet another person knowledgeable in the medical field. After hearing the details of Darrell's medical situation, they would often say the same thing, "Your husband should not be alive!" They were right; my husband is a living miracle who was spared by the powerful grace of God in a modern-day battle between good and evil.

Finally, and most importantly, if any person reading this book desires to utter any praise, may it all go to God. You will soon see that He performed some amazingly spectacular works for us, and we want the honor to go to Him. To those reading our story who might not know God in a close, personal way, my prayer is that you will see what a loving Heavenly Father He was to us. You can also have confidence to trust Him with everything, including your eternal security.

CHAPTER ONE

"You Want to Go to Eden Too?!"

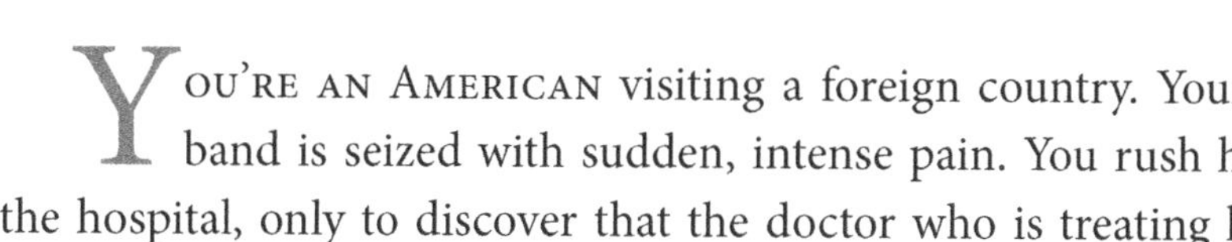

YOU'RE AN AMERICAN visiting a foreign country. Your husband is seized with sudden, intense pain. You rush him to the hospital, only to discover that the doctor who is treating him is clearly anti-American. Before long your husband is at the brink of death—due to the doctor's intentional neglect. That day your husband is ushered into a perfectly peaceful realm he can only describe as being, "Halfway to Heaven." How can you experience events such as these and not share how God miraculously intervened on your behalf? The short answer is, *you can't.*

Being in harm's way was not unknown to my husband. While on active-duty service and while taking previous mission trips, Darrell had experienced some rather close calls with danger:

- While serving multiple tours of duty during Operation Desert Thunder and Operation Desert Fox, Darrell watched as planes took off, knowing they were on a mission to bomb Iraq. These Middle Eastern deployments were carried out during the time when retaliatory threats were made of unleashing chemical weapons against our troops.
- "Go! You must leave now!" Imagine the surprise of being kicked out of a hotel in Pakistan after being there for only a few hours. While Darrell was in Pakistan, the terrorist bombings were quickly intensifying, so much so that the hotel owners were afraid to house Americans.

- Imagine proudly taking a picture of the American flag at the U.S. Embassy in Bangladesh and instantly being surrounded by five different groups of law enforcement. One of the groups is a force of black-garbed men bursting from the back of a van with assault rifles in hand. Then imagine the relief of being released after an hour and a half of intense questioning.
- Imagine setting up a film to show to a group of villagers in Myanmar and discovering the authorities have been notified and are coming after you. Imagine being told to flee immediately, but the only avenue of escape is to flag down a young man who is passing by…on a bicycle…with three additional passengers!

These brief examples illustrate how Darrell was spared from bodily harm while he was serving in the military and on the mission field. Even more so, the particular set of events I am about to share required the intervening hand of God to spare the life of my husband.

In case you are asking yourself after reading this chapter's title, "Is there really a country named Eden?" No, there is not. As I stated in the preface, I am not naming the partially Communist country where we were for the safety of those American missionaries who still live there. Rather, I will use this fictitious name for the duration of the book.

Darrell and his traveling companion, Tom, spent many weeks planning a 28-day mission trip to three Asian countries during the summer of 2011. They were disappointed to cancel going to Pakistan (which would have been their second time being there) as part of their trip. When our United States forces killed Osama Bin Laden near Islamabad, Pakistan just a few months earlier, we knew this was not the time for a retired Air Force officer (or any American for that matter) to be traveling to that country.

Originally, Darrell was planning to travel with Tom to Eden for eight days and then travel to southern India to work with a pastor who operates an orphanage. After that I was to meet them in Northeast India for nine days before heading to Bangkok, Thailand, to minister with a Thai pastor and his family for a week.

"You want to go to Eden, too?!" With a confused look on his face, Darrell asked this chapter title-worthy question when I surprised him by saying that I felt like I should go to Eden, making it a four-week, three-country trip for me as well. Thankfully, Darrell agreed with my unexpected request to join them and travel the entire trip together. This change of plans was truly divine as we had no idea how critical it would be for me to be with my husband in that foreign land. I had never traveled that far in my life, purposefully. Having had a spinal fusion that added five pounds of steel reinforcement to my back, a ruptured disc, osteoarthritis, and a lifting limitation of ten pounds, I was not the ideal long-distance traveler. Putting aside my desire to go, I asked my pastor to pray for wisdom if I should continue with our plans for me to go on the trip, as we wanted to avoid serious risks associated with my back. After praying daily, he never discovered a reason for me not to go. So with a "green light" from Pastor Hall, and peace through our own prayers, we bought the tickets.

What makes this part of our story so incredible is that Darrell has said for years that I should never travel to Asia; it was simply too far, especially with my spine surgeon saying I should not sit longer than 30 minutes. But God put that desire on my heart as a part of His perfect plan. Little did we know that day in April how badly my husband would need me every day from the end of July until the middle of September.

April began our important checklist of things that needed to be done. Shot records were brought up-to-date, prescriptions were filled for my back pain medications, airline and hotel reservations were made, and our ministry and speaking schedules were confirmed. I laminated English lessons to teach hundreds, if not thousands, of students, and I gathered spices to show the Indian people how to make American BBQ (at their request).

We coordinated with our neighbor Rose, who took care of the daily needs at our home and we prepared our business for our month-long expedition. We met with Jennifer, our shipping manager, and friends, Juan and Angie, to take care of the financial responsibilities that would come up while we were away. In order to do so, we had to share personal information such as passwords, sales figures, etc., which isn't something we would normally divulge. In all honesty, I wasn't that comfortable with what lengths we had to go, but we really had no choice.

As it turned out, God amazingly had His hand in this venture—long before we ever boarded a plane.

CHAPTER TWO

"T-Minus Ten Days…and So Much to Do!"

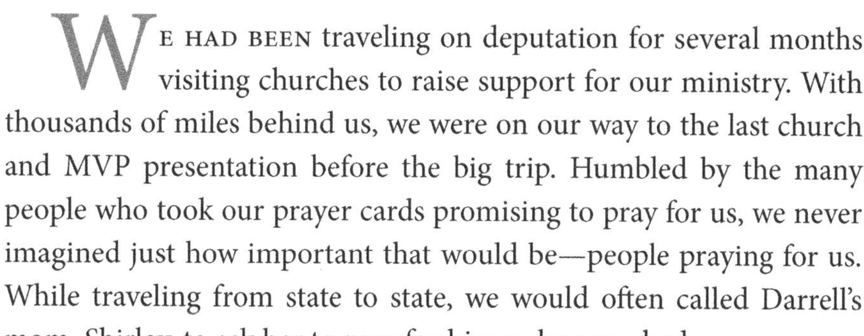

WE HAD BEEN traveling on deputation for several months visiting churches to raise support for our ministry. With thousands of miles behind us, we were on our way to the last church and MVP presentation before the big trip. Humbled by the many people who took our prayer cards promising to pray for us, we never imagined just how important that would be—people praying for us. While traveling from state to state, we would often called Darrell's mom, Shirley, to ask her to pray for him as he preached.

We were humbled once again as some of the churches, as well as a few individuals, offered their financial support to help with the expenses of our upcoming trip. The financial support was a blessing because years of primarily self-funding had depleted most of our personal savings. One day in Heaven, when we gaze upon the beautiful faces of those we helped lead to the Lord, we will consider any physical pain we've endured and the money spent well worth the cost.

Shortly before our trip, we received another unexpected blessing. A trade magazine wanted to feature me in an article called, "Women of Towing" because of our involvement in the towing industry since 1986. Imagine my delight when the editors also wanted to do a second article on our MVP Missions' ministry!

Darrell and I were so excited about the opportunity that I couldn't wait to call my mom, Carol, to get more details on the towing business that her parents/my grandparents once owned. Mom and I had the most precious phone conversation. I was tickled and comforted to hear her joyfully reminisce during our conversation as she had not been feeling well for the last few months. I had been quite concerned about her as she had recently lost a significant amount of weight.

Mom told me how she and Daddy had met and fallen in love as teenagers, while he worked for her dad's towing company in California. She shared stories of her grade school years with Dad and of family dinners together—details I had never before heard. She was so happy that day, and so were we! Our hearts were warmed to hear her speak so openly, and of course, we were thrilled to be interviewed by a secular trade magazine that wanted to run an article about our mission trips!

After the magazine interview, we headed south to the Port Charlotte, Florida, area before leaving the country. We enjoyed attending the church there and the visit with our hosts, Bob and Sherryl, a sweet, retired couple whom Darrell had met on a mission trip two years earlier in Antigua.

After the service, we were excited to head home the following morning for the final six days of preparation for the big event, the 47 hours of travel to our first overseas destination.

Squelching some of that excitement, Darrell had an upset stomach, requiring him to get up a few times during the night to visit the restroom. He thought it was simply an upset stomach or mild food poisoning because we had eaten in several restaurants while traveling. After taking Pepto-Bismol® in the morning, Darrell felt well enough to drive the seven hours home, taking a break about halfway home.

Early that evening when we pulled into the garage, Darrell took some more Pepto-Bismol® and went straight to bed for the night. While unloading the car by myself, I wondered "What on earth did the poor man eat that made him so sick?"

At this point let me backtrack and share some pertinent medical history. Darrell had experienced two mild bouts of diverticulitis[1]—one in the summer of 2009, and another in the summer of 2010. The episodes were not painful, and he described the feeling as "having a small water balloon on the left side of my abdomen."

To him, this new sickness did not feel like his two previous experiences with diverticulitis; hence, our assumption that it was most likely food poisoning. Darrell awoke Friday morning to the same mild pain, but by now he was running a low-grade fever. I researched the Internet looking for information on the symptoms of both diverticulitis and food poisoning. His symptoms did not seem to fit food poisoning as they are usually more severe.

Our doctor's office is so close we could walk to it, so I suggested that he make an appointment to see Mary Jo, our PA. Darrell didn't feel the need to go for two months earlier he had received a clean bill of health regarding his diverticulitis. After multiple referrals, blood work, an ultrasound, and a colonoscopy, the doctors had told him, "You are fine, see you in ten years!" He left the office with no follow-up appointments or diet restrictions—although we both decided to ban sunflower seeds to be on the safe side. The onset of his previous mild episodes came after eating an abundance of sunflower seeds.

We continued to treat Darrell as per the advice from multiple medical websites: liquid diet, rest, and if the pain became severe, seek medical help. Friday became a clear-soup-and-bouillon day while Darrell rested and looked over his sermon notes for the mission trip.

Saturday morning Darrell woke me up early and told me he wanted to drive himself to the emergency room. Overnight he reconsidered my concern about being checked by a doctor, and now he wanted to go to the hospital. Shocked by his announcement, I asked if I could first take his temperature, considering his ability to make the trip alone as the ER was not at the end of our street, but about 25 minutes away in the next city.

With his pain still at a minimal level, I called Darrell's mom and other friends for advice on their personal bouts with diverticulitis. They confirmed what many websites suggested: go to the hospital when the pain is severe. Since Darrell's pain was far from severe, we both decided to keep up the home treatment of the liquid diet and rest.

By Saturday afternoon his fever was gone, and his pain level was waning. On Sunday, he was totally pain and fever-free, so we both went to church. He volunteered on his own to keep up with a liquid diet while we continued to work on preparations for the big trip on Wednesday.

Monday afternoon, while Darrell was out running errands, I had a nagging thought; "Fever is often a sign of infection." Unable to shake that thought, I called the doctor's office and talked to Mary Jo. After I explained what had been happening with Darrell, she indicated she would be happy to fit him in that day.

Happily walking in the door from concluding his errands, Darrell was greeted with, "Mary Jo would be glad to see you today in case you needed antibiotics." But by now he was feeling great—no pain or fever for two days. He did not want to go, and…I did not force him.

From this experience I have learned the truth of the following sayings:

- "It *is* [quite] easy to play Monday morning quarterback."
- "Hindsight is [*always*] 20/20."

That day he looked and felt fine; but oh, how I wish I had insisted he go.

---

[1]*diverticulitis:* small, bulging sacs or pouches of the inner lining of the intestines that can become inflamed or infected.

CHAPTER THREE

The Longest Night I Remember

WORDS CANNOT DESCRIBE how excited I was about the amazing adventure to begin in the morning—my first trip to Asia. After finishing last minute preparations, I slipped quietly into bed, careful not to disturb my sleeping husband. As tired as my body was, I could not fall sleep. I tossed and turned until I was afraid I would awaken Darrell!

Feeling a restlessness in my spirit, I decided to pray in generalities, hoping to ease my mind. Disappointed when that tactic didn't work, I laid awake for hours with an unsettled feeling. I think I dozed for about 45 minutes, at best.

When my spirit feels troubled in the middle of the night, I usually check my email and Facebook. Nearly every time I do, I find that someone has asked for a specific prayer request. I kept resisting the urge to get out of bed knowing I had a 47-hour journey ahead of me.

Frustrated with tossing and turning, I finally surrendered before the alarm clock sounded. I quietly got out of bed to check my email and indeed found someone to pray for—it was my mom. While I was in bed turning like a rotisserie chicken, my siblings in California were emailing about how Mom was getting weak.

This had happened once before, but she felt better after receiving intravenous (IV) fluids at the hospital. My siblings decided the time had come to take her to the hospital again. Four o'clock in the morning was not the time to call anyone, so I simply prayed for my mom as I prepared for the trip a little earlier than I planned.

A few hours later, Darrell and I were at the airport and made our first of five connections to Eden. Since our layover in Atlanta was several hours long, I had time to call my mom. During our first flight Darrell and I discussed giving my mom "veto power" over our trip, meaning if she wanted me to be with her in California, I would immediately change my travel plans. When I called and made that offer, she replied without hesitation, "No honey, what you and Darrell are doing is important. No, please go on your mission trip. They will give me the IV fluids, and I will feel better—just like last time."

Two weeks earlier I had been willing to fly to California to be with her for one of her medical tests, but she did not want me to fly across the country and back with our long overseas trip quickly approaching. She was so sweet to be concerned about my back issues, while I had my own concerns for her health.

I asked her one more time if she wanted me to come to California, and she replied very clearly that she wanted me to go on the trip. Before saying goodbye, I told her how excited I was for our upcoming trip to California in September, and I told her that I loved her. She sounded tired, but she was happy that we were able to talk one more time before Darrell and I left the country. I loved hearing her voice before our long flight across the ocean.

As it turned out, Mom's declining my offer to be with her was instrumental in saving my husband's life. My being with Darrell was an absolute necessity; we simply didn't know it yet.

The first few flights were smooth; and after nearly 30 hours of travel, we met up with our traveling companion, Tom, in Thailand. After retrieving our luggage and going through customs, the three of us were in good spirits and excited to get to Eden.

As we prepared to check our bags for our next flight to India, we learned that every one of our bags were overweight! This flight was with a different airline, so they had different weight limitations. We were both surprised and disappointed to learn we would have to pay fees for overweight baggage. Also, Tom had brought an extra bag, which he knew would incur an additional fee.

While the agent at the counter was calculating our fees, I mentioned that we were missionaries and that we were carrying toys in our suitcases for the orphans we would be visiting in India. Before I could finish my sentence, she stopped calculating and looked at me with a smile. In a kind-hearted gesture, she waived ALL of the fees for ALL our bags! I thanked God over and over for that wonderful blessing.

During our layover in Bangkok, I used Tom's computer to call my mom via Skype. After checking email and not finding an update about her condition, I thought I would try to reach her at home. As much as she and I had talked before the trip, I forgot to tell her I was carrying the Thomas Kinkade Bible cover she had given me. I generally don't use Bible covers, but I really needed one for this trip. Inside the cover I had placed the items I would need while teaching the ladies' classes overseas: a cross-stitch picture, my lesson notes, and many copies of a picture of a toucan.

We had encountered the toucan on a previous trip out of the country. The beautifully colored bird with bright blue feet had been an answer to prayer and had actually flown down and hopped over to Darrell, even playing with his camera strap! Everything I needed fit perfectly in the Bible cover, and I was so excited to tell her. Since there was no answer at her house, I left a message telling her that I was in Thailand, that I hoped she was feeling better, and that I loved her.

Our flight took us to India for our final layover. There I discovered that being a blonde really paid off. The three of us got off the plane and started to walk...and walk...and walk! I was walking ahead of the men when a man in an airport passenger cart pulled up and said, "Ma'am, do you need a ride?"

This "Ma'am" happens to like to walk, so I started to shake my head, "No," when Tom stepped up and hopped into the cart. Good thing he did because we had no idea how far we were going to have to walk until the driver drove...and drove...and drove! Apparently, the driver did not notice anyone else among the stream of passengers deplaning, including a man walking slowly with two arm crutches directly ahead of us. He only spied the blonde.

We were on our last flight when Darrell had his first solid food since starting his liquid diet—curried meat and rice. He ate the rice and a little bit of the mystery meat, which I am sure was not a favorite first meal.

We landed safely at our final destination in the early evening. For the first time we met our host missionary, his wife, and their teenage son—Wayne, Louise, and Jeremy (fictitious names). We stopped for a quick bite at a fast-food restaurant while we enjoyed getting to know each other.

As we drove to their home, I enjoyed the views, and it was apparent that we were in a tropical setting. With dusk approaching, large, black birds appeared in the sky, each one carefully searching the treetops before descending into his preferred spot for the night. Even as they were settling down, large, black bats began to emerge, flapping their way from the same trees for their night of flight. What a thrill it was to witness the world's most bizarre shift change!

We arrived safely at our host's lovely home, and after nearly two full days of travel, Darrell and I were more than ready to settle into their comfortable guest room for the night.

CHAPTER FOUR

Day 1—Extreme Highs and Extreme Lows

We awakened to unfamiliar, yet glorious melodies from the birds of Eden. As we sipped our coffee, we enjoyed the tropical beauty outside the front door. Beautiful, lush green plants with coconut and palm trees were seen in all directions. We were glad to be feeling so well after multiple days of travel.

After the Saturday morning prayer meeting at church, Tom traveled with another pastor into the mountains to another church a few hours away. I went to a ladies' prayer meeting and was thrilled to hear people praying in three different languages!

The men and ladies split into groups to go around town and distribute gospel tracts.[1] With part of Eden's government being communist, the people do not have the same freedoms regarding religion that are enjoyed in the United States.

As we made our way onto the main street, I was wide-eyed as we viewed the sights of a busy Asian town. Suddenly, I noticed something peculiar take place. As a fair-skinned blonde, I really stood out in this dark-skinned nation. The taxi drivers noticed me and would veer across all lanes of traffic, pull over beside me, and ask, "What are you doing here?"

Smiling, I said, "I came all the way from America to give this to you!" as I handed the driver a gospel tract. These drivers happily took them every time. I was thrilled at this unexpected opportunity, and I was even able to speak about the Bible to two people who were walking on the side of the street. I was able to talk to them about knowing that they could have a home in Heaven. Louise, the missionary's wife, taught me how to recognize a Muslim person by their clothing so I could hand out the appropriate tract in their language.

The weather was extremely hot, so I welcomed a short-lived torrential downpour which is common during the monsoon season. Although I was soaked, I was happy to experience such exciting adventures on my first day. The rain quickly ceased, and due to the scorching heat, our clothes were nearly dry by the time we arrived back at the church.

While we waited for the men to return, I noticed an older man sitting at the front of the church property. His clothes were worn and dirty, and I could tell by the way he was seated that he was handicapped. I went to greet him and while reaching toward his shoulder, Louise quickly said, "You better not touch him; he might be a leper."

I was shocked to hear that word, as leprosy was a disease I had only read about in the Bible.

As the crippled man started to leave, I saw that a leg deformity prevented him from walking. He was forced to crawl away on all fours, but with his torso facing up. Slowly and awkwardly, with shoes on his hands, this dear man scooted away. My heart broke that he was alone, poor and handicapped, and I could do nothing for him. When the men returned, I shared with Darrell the many things I had experienced.

The people of the church were very kind, thanking us repeatedly for coming to be with them. I loved the warm way the women greeted each other. They put their cheek against your cheek, quickly switching to the other cheek, often making a kissing sound. Each greeting was genuine; I could feel it.

We sat down to eat a curry lunch provided by the church. I was excited to taste something new when I was suddenly wide-eyed, thrust into an, "I-should-not-be-staring" situation. The gentle people of this country do not use utensils. They were eating curry chicken, rice, gravy, and a vegetable puree with a "scoop" they made by curling their three center fingers. They ate their food very quickly, and I was trying hard not to stare. As I wondered how I was going to eat with my long fingernails, I was relieved when Louise provided forks for us to use.

Unbeknownst to me, Darrell felt like the curry might not have settled very well with him. But after a liquid diet for a week and then eating spicy, foreign food, an unsettled stomach seemed rather expected.

Darrell recently told me how bad he truly felt that day. He said he felt something inside his stomach "clamp down" really hard. When he went to the restroom, he couldn't urinate. He had to sit down and purposely relax for nearly 15 minutes before he could go to the bathroom.

(This paragraph is off the subject, but speaking of bathrooms, I was thankful for a husband who was a veteran on the mission field. He had instructed me to always carry bathroom tissue. When I entered the restroom, I learned another fascinating facet about Eden's culture. In lieu of toilet tissue, a spray hose is provided next to the commode. And as I mentioned before, I was very thankful Darrell had taught me to be prepared!)

After an enjoyable time with the church members, we said goodbye as we prepared to go back to Wayne and Louise's home. We had such a fulfilling day!

While driving to their home, we saw skinny dogs, cows, and water buffalo—standing or walking in the middle of the road! At times, Wayne had to carefully weave the car around these large animals.

Once home, we were visiting in the kitchen when we were rudely interrupted—by monkeys noisily climbing on their roof!! Grabbing our cameras, Darrell and I raced outside to take pictures until they disappeared into the trees. We also saw a large, three-foot monitor sunning on the grass.

When the excitement from seeing the monkeys died down, Darrell said he wanted to look over his notes for Sunday's messages because he was scheduled to preach four times that day. He was very excited for the opportunities there in Eden. He also planned to rest a bit—my sweet husband, lover of naps.

While Darrell studied and rested, I prepared to make dinner. I love to cook, and I enjoy sharing recipes with missionaries we meet. Louise helped me gather ingredients so I could prepare one of our favorite dinners—honey-spiced chicken and pasta alfredo.

Feeling so good that afternoon despite all the recent traveling, I didn't need a nap. I kept busy doing lots of little tasks. I glanced over my lesson for the ladies' Sunday school class the next morning, I started dinner, and I updated my Facebook page to inform everyone that we had arrived safely. I shared the events of our first day of ministry and thanked them for their prayers for traveling safety, and especially for the specific prayers for my back because I felt fantastic.

When I did not see any news about my mom, I emailed my siblings asking for an update. Thankfully, I got a reply fairly soon that Mom was still in the hospital. I was glad to finally know where she was.

While I was cooking, Wayne kept saying I would "crash with jet lag" but I never did. Lots of prayers and a little melatonin on the flights seemed to help. I needed a break from cooking in the heat of the day, so I went to cool down in our air-conditioned bedroom where Darrell was studying and possibly resting.

When I walked into the room, Darrell was standing with one hand holding himself up at the desk, the other hand holding his lower abdomen. When I asked him what was wrong, he indicated he was having some pain. With dinner almost done, I had to run between our bedroom and the kitchen. Each time I checked on Darrell, his pain seemed to be a little worse.

About five minutes before dinner was ready, Darrell was in so much pain that we all agreed he needed medical care. This pain was like nothing he had ever experienced in his life. The pain was centralized and shooting straight down through the center of his abdomen. Nothing hurt on the left or the right side. We wondered if he had kidney stones because of the location and the intermittent, severe pain he was experiencing. The gripping pain would come and go without any warning.

Wayne took Darrell to the hospital while I stayed back to finish dinner, all the while earnestly praying for my husband. I quickly sent out a prayer request for Darrell on Facebook, also mentioning that my mom was still in the hospital.

The hospital staff immediately gave Darrell a shot for pain and drew blood. Thankfully, his pain started to subside. The hospital personnel offered to admit him, but with his pain easing, he wanted to return to the house. Darrell was given some oral pain medication, and the two hungry men returned home.

The shot allowed Darrell to sit down and eat a hearty meal with the rest of us. Everyone seemed to be exhausted from Darrell's frightening ordeal, so we decided to call it a night. My husband and I retired to our room, but very soon the pain returned—this time, with a vengeance.

Darrell immediately took the pain pills he had been given at the hospital. However, even with ample time, there was no relief at all. Darrell described his pain: "I feel as if lightening is trying to shoot straight out of me." He said the agonizing pain went from his stomach, straight down, and seemingly "through and out" of his body.

The pain was so strong, Darrell had no choice but to lie on the bed and literally twist the sheets with his hands in agony. I was grieved to even watch. Both Darrell and I knew he had to go back to the hospital, so with a frightened heart, I climbed the dark, winding stairway to awaken Wayne.

I asked Darrell if I could go to the hospital with him, but he said, "No, you came here to teach the ladies, and you need to do that. That is why we came." I understood; but I really wanted to be with my husband.

Wayne handed me one of their cell phones so he could text me updates. As they got into the car, Darrell was tightly clutching the decorative pillow that had once graced our bed. He could not let go of that pillow for the pain raging in his body. My heart ached as they drove away.

Earlier, Wayne had made the decision to send Tom to the mountain church, which meant he was separated from the hospital by a three-hour drive of winding roads. Had he sent us to that area instead, Darrell would have had to endure that grueling, long car ride while being racked with excruciating pain. We are so thankful that God put it on Wayne's heart to have us stay in their home, which was much closer to the hospital.

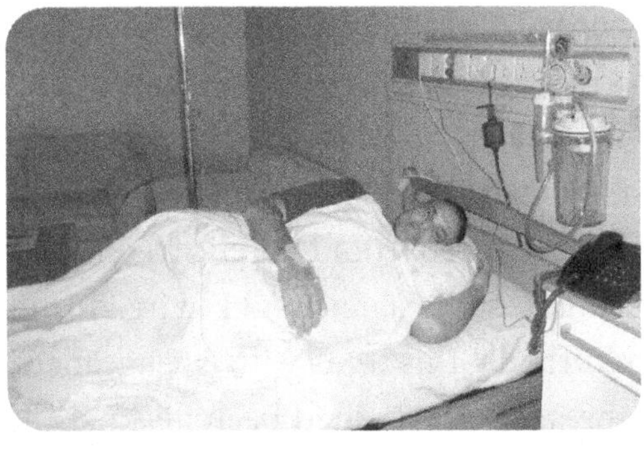

I sent an urgent email and posted a Facebook update, asking everyone to pray for Darrell. After praying, I tried to go to sleep. But how was I going to fall asleep when just moments earlier my husband was lying in the same bed—writhing in sheet-twisting pain? There I was, doing the dreadful "toss and turn" once again. I decided if I couldn't fall asleep, I might as well get up and glance over the lesson I was about to teach in the morning.

Wow, what timing! Little did I know when I was preparing my lesson months before, that I would need to cling to the very verses that were in it! There they were—all written out and ready for me to read. I was in awe that God would be so kind as to have something I *truly* needed already prepared in advance. His provision for me in that moment was perfect.

---

[1]*tract*: a small paper, usually folded, that has a clear Bible plan of salvation.

CHAPTER FIVE

A Very Busy Day of Rest

BECAUSE OF GROWING concern for my husband and my continuing to check the phone for updates, I found it difficult to fall asleep. The first text I received from Wayne indicated that the hospital staff was doing blood work. After some time had passed, a second text arrived telling me that Darrell was being admitted.

While lying in my warm, comfortable bed, I imagined my husband alone in the cold, sterile environment of a hospital. I felt a twinge of guilt because I was not with him, but knowing he was now under the watchful care of the doctors, I was finally able to doze off.

Shortly after 2:00 a.m., I was jolted out of sleep, remembering Darrell still had his wallet. That wallet had all of the money for our nearly month-long mission trip! We had made the decision to travel with cash because many countries will no longer accept traveler's checks. Since there was nothing I could do about it at that hour, I prayed and asked God to protect my husband, and his wallet.

I awoke again at 3:00 a.m. though I wasn't sure why. I simply prayed again for Darrell and my mom. Unintentionally, I perfected another nearly sleepless night, and Sunday morning surely came quickly.

That morning I perked up when Louise told me we could stop by the hospital on the way to church. Although our visit was short, I was so relieved to see Darrell. He shared with me that after he was admitted and given a shot for pain, a male nurse wheeled him into a room, turned off the light, and said, "Goodnight." The nurse did not bother to show Darrell where the call button was should he need any help.

Resting alone in the dark, Darrell started to feel the twinges of pain return.

Fearful that the pain would escalate, my husband looked everywhere for the call button to signal for help. He could not find the pager anywhere, so he used the phone next to his bed to call the switchboard operator to send for help. However, the person who answered the phone spoke very little English. Darrell asked the operator to have a nurse come to his room; but after a period of time, it became apparent that nobody was coming. He called the operator a few more times in an attempt to reach a nurse.

Finally, Darrell heard a phone ringing at the nurses' station not far from his room. Unfortunately, nobody answered. The operator tried calling the nurses' station a few more times, but there never was an answer. Hearing what had happened to him broke my heart. Thankfully, Darrell said his pain was mostly bearable.

When he said this happened at 3:00 a.m., I instantly knew why I had awakened at that hour. I am glad the Holy Spirit will gently nudge us awake when He wants us to pray for someone. Many of our friends shared how they too felt as if God had awakened them at different times, and when they checked their computer, they found we were facing a critical situation needing fervent prayer. God's watch-care is truly amazing!

After leaving Darrell, I was happy to walk into church and see the ladies and teenagers I had met the previous day. They welcomed me warmly with their beautiful smiles and unique cheek-to-cheek greetings.

Before I started my lesson, Louise asked one of the ladies to pray and ask the Lord to bless the morning class. Surprisingly, as Louise gave her specific matters for which to pray, the lady began to shake her head, side to side (imagine someone quickly putting his ears toward their shoulders). As she continued to rock her head back and forth, I became more and more embarrassed for her. After all, many people are uncomfortable when asked to pray out loud in a group setting; but I felt badly for her because she was being asked to pray in front of the American guest speaker. In this extremely awkward moment, I prayed for her silently. Then, all of a sudden, she started to pray!

I was confused because I thought she was saying she didn't want to pray, but I had to quickly focus on my lesson. I stored the event in the back of my mind and decided to ask Louise about it later when we were alone.

Using a translator for the first time was exciting. The ladies were attentive to the lesson, and Louise said the class had a near-record attendance—maybe due in part to their curiosity in having an American visitor. As I began to teach my lesson on trust, I realized Darrell being in the hospital in a third-world country was a perfect example of what I was teaching. The ladies shared kind words about the lesson, and I have kept their precious handwritten notes to this day.

Apparently, Wayne had shared with the men's class that Darrell had been admitted to the hospital. I was comforted by so many people telling me that they were praying for him. Since three different languages are spoken in Eden, the church holds multiple services to accommodate everyone who wants to go to their church. I thoroughly enjoyed the services that day.

After a wonderful lunch, Wayne and Louise took me back to their house so I could pack some necessities. I planned to move into that hospital because I could not—would not—let Darrell go another night without pain medicine or a nurse's visit.

Although tired, I remembered to ask Louise about the bizarre praying incident that occurred earlier that morning. Laughing, Louise explained that the people use that odd head shake to indicate "Yes." To me, it looked more negative than positive, hence my confusion. The best way to picture their unique head wag is to visualize the movement of a Bobble-head doll rocking ear-side to ear-side. It's actually quite cute!

Not knowing whether the hospital would have Internet service, I quickly checked my email for updates on my mom. I found no updates; however, some of my siblings sent notes requesting that I not mention Mom openly on Facebook. I apologized right away for my post; I didn't realize they wanted the situation kept private. I then hurried to pack my things, and we headed to the hospital.

After placing my suitcase in the corner of Darrell's room, I sat on the sofa close to where he lay. I realized that my tall husband did not fit very well in the bed. Neither did he fit in their hospital gowns… once they finally gave him one—which was on Wednesday! He had to leave an arm out of the sleeve because the gowns were so small that the armholes cut-off his circulation.

Our "new home" was unlike any hospital room we had ever seen. Black mold, which is not good for anyone—especially for those who are already sick, grew in the corner of the room. Nurses used the old-fashioned type of blood pressure (BP) cuff. As the rubber bulb is squeezed, the mercury slowly rises; readings are taken as the mercury recedes. A mercury thermometer was also used, and it was wiped with rubbing alcohol right before they put it into his mouth.

It did not matter that the equipment around his bed was old, because it was not used. I felt like we had taken a time machine back 30 years. There was no electronic equipment attached to Darrell to alert the nurses of a serious problem. The BP cuff was built into an old metal box which squeaked loudly when the nurse opened and closed it.

My bed was very firm and was placed across the room in a corner by the door. Although the room was badly in need of a mop and some bleach water, it was large and had a little balcony. Words cannot express how much I loved our little balcony, which would become my personal retreat—the quiet place to where I would escape when I needed to pray.

I could devote an entire chapter to the air conditioning system. Because the thermostat did not work, it had only one setting: Arctic cold, with a wind force teetering on a category-one hurricane. We can now laugh about our comical A/C escapades. Because Darrell was losing weight, he chilled easily. The weather outside was much hotter than what we were accustomed because we were closer to the equator. When Darrell got hot, he would ask, "Honey, can you please turn on the air?" I would turn the air on for him, and within 30 minutes, he was freezing. He would then say, "Honey, can you please turn off the air?" After another 20 to 30 minutes he would say, "Honey, it's really hot. Can you please turn on the air?"

This cycle continued throughout our stay. Thankfully, the nights cooled down enough so I did not have to turn on the air. Darrell felt bad for continually asking me to turn on and off the air system, but I was happy to help. Not only did fulfilling his requests give me something to do, but I also experienced the same extreme temperature changes.

The air situation alone made me thankful I was with Darrell on this trip, as he never would have called the nurses to adjust the air each time he was uncomfortable. And...quite possibly, they would not have understood him anyway.

CHAPTER SIX

An Arrogant First Impression

As Darrell's pain became more intense, I had to go alert one of the nurses at the nurses' station. She came to the room and gave Darrell a pain pill. Unfortunately, that medication did not work, and very shortly he was again writhing in pain.

I ran back to tell the nurse, and she came to our room and immediately gave Darrell a shot. I really hated to see him in that much pain.

After that stressful episode, I needed my three-minute balcony break. Stepping outside, I took a deep breath, said a prayer, and looked for birds. God knew my need and He sent a beauty.

In the very difficult times of my life, I would see a special bird that I knew God had sent. They were either special in beauty or special in such a way as to make me laugh. God was good to me in many little, yet profound, ways.

The nurses periodically came to softly ask Darrell how he was feeling. After nearly an hour with little relief, the nurse gave him a second shot. At this point, I believe the nurse upgraded his IV medication because once she changed the bag, his pain was under control. What a relief it was. He didn't need shots after that. Due to the language barrier, I could not ask what medication was being administered. However, to see him go from writhing in pain to resting comfortably, I knew the medication had to be something strong.

Over the next few hours, it was good to see Darrell finally relax and take his normal Sunday afternoon nap. Later that day, we finally got to meet the doctor. He was a little taller than most of the local men, and he did not seem very friendly, which was in stark contrast to the many sweet people we had already met. He asked why we were in his country, and not knowing that Eden was a partially communist country and "closed" regarding the Gospel, we ignorantly told him we were missionaries.

He then asked Darrell what type of work he did back home. Again, not knowing there was strife between our nations, he shared that he was a retired Air Force officer. (We suspect he asked the work question because Darrell was wearing his USAF t-shirt.)

Unknowingly, we gave this doctor two strong reasons to dislike his new patient. This aversion was evidenced by his frequent criticism of our nation and also by his mannerisms. His arms were crossed high and tight across his chest, and he made repeated, disparaging sighs. He acted more bothered than helpful, and this haughtiness was only the beginning of his mistreatment of my husband.

Darrell was admitted to the hospital late Saturday night. Sunday afternoon, when we finally spoke to the doctor, he declared, "We do not do any testing on Sundays." Darrell needed a CAT scan but would have to wait until Monday. I found it hard to believe that a predominantly Buddhist nation would honor the Lord's Day and fail to perform procedures necessary to save a person's life.

After experiencing the doctor's negative attitude and mannerisms, I watched everything he did like a hawk. The doctor pushed on Darrell's abdomen, and it did not seem to hurt very much. As the doctor pressed, he asked, "Does this hurt?"

Darrell would say, "A little."

Pushing on another spot, he asked, "Does this hurt?"

"Not really."

Looking back now, I must wonder if the strong IV medicines he was taking masked the tenderness he might have otherwise felt. The pain management was probably the best medical care he received at that hospital.

The doctor told us the blood work from Saturday night showed Darrell's white blood cell count was in the normal range, but his C-reactive protein (CRP)[1] levels were elevated. The doctor also said that Darrell's temperature was not considered high.

At that point, the three of us discussed releasing Darrell, which would save us the overnight hospital fees. We could then come back on Monday for the CAT scan.

Because of the doctor's lackadaisical attitude, we temporarily forgot how much pain Darrell had felt—the very reason we took him to the hospital in the first place. Once that IV was removed, the raging pain would have come back. I am so glad we decided not to leave!

---

[1]CRP measures levels of inflammation, which when elevated, can indicate infection.

CHAPTER SEVEN

Treatment...and Mistreatment Begin

THE NEXT MORNING, we were shocked to be awakened at 5:30 a.m. by an hour-long chant broadcasted by the local Buddhist temple over loudspeakers. The once-sleeping birds in the tree-lined park across from our balcony quickly began to protest as loud as or louder than the amped-up chants.

I loved hearing their assorted tropical calls. One particular cry was, "Whoop whoop whoop whoop!" Each consecutive whoop was a pitch higher than the previous one. I loved hearing Eden's amazing birds—which I never knew existed until this trip.

I envisioned the birds vehemently declaring to the world that they knew it was God Who had created them—not an idol. I also felt like they were as annoyed as I was to be awakened so abruptly at 5:30 a.m.! The hospital staff brought tea to the patients' rooms at about 6:00 a.m. daily. Days start early in Eden.

Wayne came to check on Darrell mid-morning on Monday. He was as frustrated as we were over the slow to non-existent care Darrell was receiving. Wayne, our new American missionary friend, is tall with a broad frame. He looks like he could play football in the NFL. He also has a booming voice, which he demonstrated as he slapped his hand on the nurses' station counter declaring, "I want answers, and I want them now!" He wanted to know why Darrell had been lying in the hospital bed since Saturday night without any testing. Next, our missionary advocate went downstairs to the hospital director's office on the first floor. He inquired about the lack of testing and also mentioned our doctor's poor bedside manner. Soon after, Darrell's first procedure was performed. When Darrell was finally taken for his CAT scan, I stayed in our room, assuming it would be a non-invasive procedure. How wrong I was!

One part of Darrell's test was so physically painful that he did not tell me about it until we were back in the United States—nearly ten months later. In fact, as I gathered details to write this book, Darrell told me more specifics of this procedure, and it left me in tears. I had no idea how badly he was treated during his CAT scan. I will share the details he revealed to me.

Darrell was taken downstairs in a wheelchair by a male nurse. Once he was in the CAT scan department, the nurse left. He was then treated by two technicians, one male and one female. They first had him change out of his street clothes that he had been wearing since Saturday night into a gown that was too small for his broad-shouldered frame. He was left to wait for a while in the small lobby. He was then called into the procedure room and the technicians had him lie face-up on the table for the scan. Darrell noticed that this room also contained old, outdated equipment.

At this point in his treatment, he had one IV port, which was most likely receiving a trifecta of fluids—antibiotics, pain medicine, and nutrients—since he was not allowed to eat. I use the words "most likely" because I am not sure he was given antibiotics at this point, even though we had been told his CRP numbers were elevated.

Once the scan started, he began to feel some warmth and a strange, pulling sensation in his arms. (When I had had a CAT scan in the States, my technician had informed me that contrast[1] would give me that sensation.) To this day, we are not sure if contrast was used in Darrell's procedure because it was never mentioned to him.

After the first scan, my husband was given a short break to fill his stomach with water. When he was finished drinking, the second scan would begin. Keep in mind that Darrell had not been allowed to drink anything orally since Saturday night. He was merely instructed to walk to a water cooler and drink five full cups of water. After not drinking anything for a couple of days, it took him almost an hour to drink such a large quantity of water.

When it was time for the second scan, “Mister Darrell” was called into the room. As he settled onto the sliding table, the male tech came to him wheeling an old, odd rectangular contraption. Darrell thought, *What a strange device.* It was constructed of metal, wood, glass, and had a hose. He could see that the piece of equipment was filled with fluid, and on one end, he saw a long wand with a handle. This sight struck Darrell with a deep feeling of horror as his mind raced through a short list of possible uses for the wand. How quickly his fears became a dreadful reality.

The tech asked Darrell to lie down and turn on his side. The tech then inserted the long wand into Darrell’s rectum. In his broken English, he explained that he was going to inject liquid for the CAT scan.

Darrell had no idea how far that wand was supposed to be inserted, but he felt like he was being tortured. Then came the liquid. So much liquid was injected that he was in excruciating pain, and he had to consciously hold it all in for the duration of the scan.

The tech had explained that the test would last only a few minutes, but Darrell (who is not one to exaggerate) told me that he cried out in agony at least 100 times for the procedure to end. He cried over and over: “Hurry! Hurry! Hurry!” and “Please be finished! Please be finished!”

Unknown to all of us at the time was his sigmoid colon[2] had ruptured. The fluids being injected into his colon sent fecal matter throughout his peritoneum.[3] We have often wondered if the excruciating pain Darrell felt during the test, brought on by that wand, is what caused his colon to rupture. That is something we will never know.

After this procedure/torture session, Darrell was directed to the bathroom. Darrell described what followed next as the worst amount of diarrhea imaginable. After more than 15 minutes, he finally was finished and physically exhausted. He was told to get dressed in his own dirty clothes, and then he was wheeled back to our room.

I was so glad to see him, and I felt relief that Darrell finally had that test done. "Now we can get some answers for what is causing his pain," I thought. Of course, I was completely oblivious to what my husband had endured as he said nothing upon entering the room. He simply laid down and slept heavily. Even after he awakened, he said nothing about the pain inflicted upon him during that procedure.

The doctor came in soon after Darrell woke up and asked him if he was hungry. Darrell gave his typical answer when offered food of any sort, "Yes!" The doctor had George, the hospital chef, bring Darrell some soup, which he ate immediately.

A short time later, the doctor came back into the room with the report from the scan. He informed us that the test showed that Darrell's peritoneum was filled with fluid and air, and that apparently something had ruptured. He added, "He has a very, very bad appendix."

Since the scan showed an enlarged appendix, the doctor suspected that it had ruptured. The doctor then said he would normally operate immediately to remove the ruptured appendix; however, he could not because Darrell had just eaten soup!

I was immediately upset at myself for not speaking up earlier. I had wanted to say to the doctor when he offered Darrell the soup, "But we don't have the CAT scan results yet. If the test determines he needs surgery and Darrell eats the soup, he will have to wait many hours, right?!"

Well, I was correct. There would be no surgery for at least seven hours. The doctor's rudeness and additional derogatory remarks about our country made me feel intimidated. I sighed a deep and regretful sigh.

Later that afternoon, Louise joined us while we waited for the surgery. The doctor returned to our room and stated factually that Darrell had appendicitis. I respectfully asked the doctor, "Do you really think it's appendicitis? He never had pain on his right side. Could he have diverticulitis?"

Louise added, "Could he possibly have peritonitis?"

Sternly, the doctor looked at both of us and in an irritable, rude tone said, "And how long have you two gone to medical school?!"

Shortly after that exchange, he left the room.

I had thought I was timid before; I now had my proverbial tail between my legs. Disappointed, we still had to wait many hours for Darrell's surgery.

I was afraid of this doctor, and I was also afraid to say anything about my fear. He was about to put Darrell under general anesthesia to operate, so I surely did not want to upset him any further. I simply had to pray silently and ask God to watch over my husband.

Apparently, while the doctor was out of our room, the director of the hospital had a talk with him. When he returned to our room, he explained the findings of the CAT scan in a less abrasive manner.

He explained that the scan did show signs of diverticulitis with inflammation, but more importantly, that it looked like a ruptured appendix. The doctor continued to explain that he would perform laparoscopic surgery[4] and that Darrell would recover quickly once his appendix was removed. The doctor concluded his explanation with some good news: after a few days of recovery, Darrell could possibly even handle the latter part of our mission trip, continuing to India and then Thailand. I clung to any good news I could get, and I wanted to share this update immediately.

Repeating the doctor's optimistic update on Facebook, I was hoping that a few days of recovery was all Darrell needed. One of my closest friends had recently had her appendix removed, and she was up and busy in no time.

Exhausted and clinging to that hope, I had to lie down for some much-needed rest. As I was about to fall asleep, I remembered that the place we planned to go to in India had no electricity. I realized that there was no way I would take Darrell, who would be recovering from surgery, to a hot, dusty country and to a place that had no air conditioning. Plus, I knew nothing about the country's standard of medical care.

Although I was already dismissing the doctor's suggestion of going to India, Darrell's frightened family did not know this fact. They thought we would entertain the doctor's "good intentions." When I awoke and checked the computer for updates, I read the deep concerns they had expressed, so I immediately reassured them that we would not be going to India.

As the situation continued to deteriorate with Darrell's doctor, my attitude changed about his concern for my husband's well-being. I don't think for a second that there ever were any "good intentions."

When we finally started to share our story some eight months later, one pastor's wife made a very strong comment. Upon hearing that the doctor had suggested Darrell could go to India so soon after having his appendix removed, she said, "I think he just wanted your husband to die."

While I do not know the doctor's motives when he suggested Darrell could travel so soon to India, he clearly proved later that he did not have Darrell's medical interest at heart.

---

[1]*Contrast*: special dye opaque to x-rays that brightens the internal organs to show up better on CAT scan x-rays

[2]*Sigmoid colon*: descending colon connecting to the rectum

[3]*Peritoneum*: internal cavity housing abdominal organs

[4]*Laparoscopic surgery*: minimally invasive surgery using a video camera and several thin instruments inserted through several small cuts

CHAPTER EIGHT

The Best Skype Call, Ever!

During the long, but necessary, wait for Darrell's soup to digest, I sent a prayer request via Facebook asking people to pray for the surgery. I also asked some family members and close friends to call Darrell's mom, Shirley, to explain that her son was facing surgery. My mother-in-law did not have a computer, so the only way for her to receive updates was by telephone. I deeply wanted us both to speak to Darrell's mom and our adult children, Darrell Jay and Bobby, before he went into surgery. Disheartened, we could not call anybody ourselves. Even though Wayne and Louise had given us a phone card, it would not work on the hospital phones. With only sporadic email, our communication was primarily through Facebook.

From the combination of too little sleep before the flights, when Darrell was in the hospital alone, our nightly nurse interruptions, and the 5:30 a.m. chanting/bird alarms, I was physically exhausted. My husband was facing surgery being performed by a rude doctor in a dirty hospital in a third-world country, relaxing was impossible. I was basically in a continuous state of prayer for Darrell. I also checked the computer often for a new update on my mom. In my tired mind, no news was *not* good news.

My bottled-up fears poured out in an emotional email to my siblings. I did not have the liberty to tell them how nervous the doctor made me feel. I was not sure if someone on the hospital staff or even our doctor could access my email, so I was careful to avoid writing anything that could potentially jeopardize my husband's health. I could only express that the lack of news about my mom's condition, along with the inability to call anyone and hear a familiar voice, left me feeling very alone. I was more than halfway around the world; at times though, it felt like I might as well been on Pluto.

Desperately longing to hear Mom's words of comfort, I accepted the fact that I was not able to speak with her. Not only did the phones fail to work, but my siblings informed me that Mom was too tired and weak to speak on the phone—even to her frightened daughter in a foreign land. They also shared that in Mom's weakened state, they dared not tell her about Darrell's medical condition, lest it upset her.

My heart ached inwardly, knowing my mom had no idea what we were experiencing. However, it ached even more that she was too weak to hear about our fragile situation.

Later that afternoon I found out that we could access Skype! However, when we finally learned it was available, it was 3:00 a.m. back home. Thankfully, a few of our friends who could not sleep went online to communicate with us. What a comfort it was to us to know they were praying!

We shared our phone dilemma online, and some friends offered to make phone calls to our sons and to Darrell's mom and sisters in the morning. Not long after providing the phone numbers, my friend, Sue, was able to reach our family.

We called Darrell's mom on the phone via Skype; and we were able to have a video chat with both of our sons before the surgery. What a blessing it was to see our children's faces! In fact, that pre-surgery Skype session allowed us to experience something incredibly special.

Our son, Darrell Jay, his wife Heather, and our 18-month-old grandson, Daniel, would pray together for us in their Pennsylvania home. They, like most of our family and friends, prayed often for Darrell. During our video call, we watched our son say to little Daniel, "Let's pray for Papa."

Daniel looked down at his pudgy little hands, and he slowly clasped them together to pray. What a comfort to see our little grandson praying for Papa halfway around the world! Once they finished praying, Daniel blew us kisses.

Since Daniel was so young, he had not yet said the words, "Nana" or "Papa." Darrell and I had gone to Pennsylvania shortly before our mission trip, and we took turns saying our own names to Daniel. Darrell would say, "Papa, Papa, Papa!" Then I would say, "Nana, Nana, Nana!" We repeated this on Skype as well. It was our little contest to see whose name he would say first. Daniel would smile whenever we played that game, but he never did repeat either of our names. After blissfully watching that little man pray and blow us kisses on the video call, we finally heard him say "Papa" for the very first time! We were absolutely delighted!

Many months later, Darrell shared how that particular Skype session with Daniel brought a special joy to his heart before his surgery. Although I can be a little competitive at times, I was thrilled that day when he said, "Papa" first.

The next few days would bring us to a place where we truly needed each and every prayer, and we know God graciously heard our little Daniel praying for his Papa.

CHAPTER NINE

The First Surgery

MONDAY CRAWLED BY and when late afternoon came, we were still waiting for surgery. Darrell took a slow, but steady, walk to the bathroom. On his way back to the bed, he put his hand on his chest saying, "I feel dizzy. It's hard to breathe."

Frightened, I jumped up to help him get into bed safely. Thankfully, he felt a little better after he laid down.

This breathing episode heightened my frustration at having to wait so long for his surgery. We were able to distract each other by discussing the wonderful Skype video calls with our sons and grandson. That afternoon, Wayne, Louise and Jeremy came to visit.

When the time for surgery finally came, a male nurse entered the room to transport Darrell on a gurney to the operating room (OR). Wayne and I planned to accompany Darrell as far as we could while Louise and Jeremey stayed behind to watch our belongings.

We walked down the hallway with the nurse pushing Darrell toward the elevator. After a short wait, we heard the *Ding!* of the elevator reaching our floor. When the doors opened, a man with a cart bearing empty juice glasses stood inside. I expected the man to exit the elevator when he saw a nurse and a patient lying on a gurney, but he didn't move. The doors closed. The nurse pushed the button again, and soon we heard another *Ding!* When the doors opened this time, I saw five nurses who looked like they had recently completed their busy shifts. I hoped they would notice the patient with an IV and an exhausted wife by his side and step out of the elevator for us. However, they did not exit the elevator, either. After pushing the button again, we patiently waited for the *Ding!* The doors opened, and this time I saw an empty gurney with a few people standing around it. Since there was not enough room for us and another gurney, the doors closed once again. He pushed the button again and shortly we heard that now familiar *Ding!* The doors opened, and there stood another man with a cart of empty juice glasses. When I saw that he was simply going to stand there, I stuck out my tiny, little foot to stop the doors from closing. With a polite request to come out of the elevator, I pulled the man's cart out into the hallway. I whisked myself into the elevator and held the doors open for the nurse to wheel Darrell in as well. Finally, we were on our way to the OR.

During our elevator ride to surgery, Wayne looked at me, and we had an unspoken exchange.

Wayne: "Did you really just do that?"

Me: "Oh, yes, I did!" We both grinned.

While I admire the politeness of the people in Eden, it was taking too long to get Darrell to the OR. I simply thought Darrell was far more important than carting away empty juice glasses.

Wayne and I stayed until Darrell was wheeled into the OR, but the waiting room was another room that needed bleach and a detailed cleaning. We returned to our hospital room which was more comfortable.

I was so glad Louise was with me during the surgery, it was more than sweet—her presence was needed. In addition to being in a constant state of prayer, I was comforted by reading the reassuring words from the emails and messages sent by those who wrote they were praying for Darrell.

The hours seemed to pass slowly. Finally, a nurse came to our room and asked us to go to the OR to see the doctor. Louise and I looked at each other somewhat bewildered. I was not prepared for this request. I have always thought it was the doctor that would come speak with the family.

Many questions arose in my mind: "Why wouldn't he come to see us?" "What could this possibly mean?" "Is my Darrell okay?!" Quietly, Louise and I walked up the stairs while I asked God to help me to be strong—no matter the outcome of the surgery.

The doctor came out and pointed at both of us saying, "You were right, and you were right." Puzzled, Louise and I looked at each other. Thus began my crash course on peritonitis[1].

The doctor explained that when he explored Darrell's abdomen with the camera, he was shocked to see the most pus and purulence[2] he had ever seen inside a patient—in his entire medical career. The doctor was stunned at the severity of Darrell's infection because he did not show the classic symptoms of peritonitis—high fever, a loss of appetite, and "come-off-the-table" pain when touched in the abdominal area. Because Darrell was most likely taking a morphine-like pain medication intravenously, that might explain why he didn't feel severe pain during the abdominal checks earlier that morning. There was certainly no lack of appetite when the doctor offered him that soup. Granted, nine or more hours had passed since that horrendous CT scan where they blasted fecal matter into his peritoneum, giving ample time for the infection to grow. The doctor showed us the pictures of the severity of the infection.

The doctor told us that he had inspected Darrell's appendix for a rupture. He turned it to the underside and then had to look it all over again. It was inflamed, but it had not burst. Confused, the doctor thought, "If it wasn't his appendix that burst, then what did?" After some exploring, he discovered that it was Darrell's sigmoid colon that had ruptured due to severe, abscessed diverticulitis. The doctor said he rinsed Darrell's abdominal area with saline, hoping that between the wash and IV antibiotics that Darrell would become strong enough to take a flight to Thailand in a few days. (We had told the doctor earlier about our missionary friends living there who told us they had excellent medical care available.) The doctor added that the alternative was a more invasive surgery which involved removing the ruptured, diseased colon, and diverting Darrell's healthy section of intestines to a colostomy bag.

After recovery, my groggy husband was wheeled back into our room. It was great to have him safely with me again. Wayne and Louise stayed a little longer to make sure we were both fine. Also, their son Jeremy never once complained about the long hours he had spent at the hospital. I thanked them for staying with me throughout the surgery, and they finally went home after a long and tiring day.

Now alone with Darrell, I could focus entirely on his recovery. It seemed that his IV had been set on turbo-drip as I had never seen a bag empty so quickly in my life! Because they had no electronic equipment to sound when a bag was empty, three times I had to run the nurses' station to let them know that it had drained completely. Almost on cue, the Lord let me wake up in the middle of the night, and as I tiptoed over to check on my sleeping husband, I would notice his IV bag was completely empty, again. I would walk wearily to the nurses' station to ask for yet another refill. Of course, the timing was always conveniently between the nurses' visits—the visits with the loud BP *squeeeeaks* and temperature checks. Oh, what I would have done for a can of WD-40®!

---

[1] *Peritonitis:* inflammation of the peritoneum, the tissue that lines the inner wall of the abdomen and covers the abdominal organs. Usually caused by a bacterial infection left untreated, peritonitis can rapidly spread into the blood (sepsis) and to other organs, resulting in multiple organ failure and death. Seeking prompt medical care upon developing any symptoms of peritonitis—the most common of which is severe abdominal pain—is imperative.

[2] *Purulence:* a festering fluid that is the product of inflammation

CHAPTER TEN

The Worst Skype Call, Ever!

During the night, a different nurse appeared for each task—one replaced the IV bag, and the other performed the BP and temperature checks. Unfortunately, they never came at the same time, which meant the lights were turned on twice as often. When we finally drifted into a good sleep, we were stirred awake by our serenading "Chanty-man" as I affectionately named him. It was good that the simultaneous squawking birds were funny because the lack of sleep was starting to show its effects on me. I looked forward to the tea service, hoping it would give me the energy I would need to tend to Darrell.

Most people complain about hospital food, but I did not. Not only did the food taste great, my meals were served on china alongside real glassware and flatware. I soon learned that I needed to stick with the "American" meal they offered. Every day the distinct aroma from the traditional curry meals wafted into the hallway in a most significant manner. I imagined my husband, who was not yet allowed to eat, would have been unhappy had I brought something so pungent smelling into our room.

As I dined alone at the table in our room, I would look at Darrell, hoping to see a recovery-glow about him, indicating the surgery was a success. Darrell seemed to be extremely quiet, but then again, he did recently have surgery. Not knowing how long it would take to see improvement, I trusted that our doctor would alert us if the less-invasive choice he had made was not working.

Next, I opened my computer and saw a fantastic message! My siblings wrote that they were going to video-call me on Skype—I was so excited! I just knew they were planning to cheer me up after they had read how far away and lonely I felt, a fact which resonated in my emails. I surely needed their moral support, with a recovering husband and my being so far away from everyone.

With a sudden surge of energy, I prepared for their call by brushing my hair, putting on mascara, brushing my teeth, and finishing with lipstick. We carefully moved Darrell to the couch, since his pain had decreased (due to the IV medications), and he also wanted to see my family on the computer with me. Additionally, it was a nice break for him after lying on the hospital bed for so many hours.

When the much-awaited call came, I was eager for our family's funny antics, but right away I noticed that they looked tired from spending long days at the hospital. Since it was quite late in California, they were more reserved than their usual fun, outgoing selves. I turned the computer so they could see Darrell sitting on the couch. They told him he looked good, considering he had recently undergone surgery. Encouraging him to get some rest and feel better, they said the typical things family members would say to a loved one in a hospital.

Then my sister, Joyce, asked, "Joanie, are you sitting down?"

I thought she was concerned about all the traveling I had done, or perhaps she was aware that I was sleeping on a hard bed. In response to her sweet request, I told her that I was fine standing.

Within a minute or so she asked again, "Are you sitting down?"

I reassured her that my back was fine, and I was more comfortable standing.

Soon she asked me a third time, "Are you sitting down?"

Concerned, I sat down at the table and leaned in close to the laptop. I looked closer at the expression on her face and then at the faces of my brothers, John and Jim. They were not sporting their typical smiles. Confused, I asked, "What's wrong?"

Awkwardly, they began to tell me things I already knew: Mom had been in the hospital because she was weak, and the doctors had been running multiple tests. Most of the tests were inconclusive; therefore, the doctor had gone ahead and performed surgery. I was surprised by the last statement, as I had no idea that my mom was going to have surgery. They told me the doctor planned to "fix" something. When the surgery was completed, the doctor indicated that Mom would not be able to breathe on her own, and that she was on oxygen. I was now more than confused; I was totally caught off guard. My lack of sleep was not helping me understand their somewhat vague conversation.

I asked, "But what if she does continue to breathe on her own?"

Their facial reactions to my question were even more confusing to me, because Darrell's mom uses oxygen at home 24/7, so I thought that if my mom needed oxygen also, that need in and of itself didn't sound very serious. Plus, my mom has always been a very strong woman. In fact, she was so strong that my dad used to bet his male friends that my mom could beat them in arm wrestling! They usually took the bet, and my mom usually won. I found it difficult to imagine that my mom was lacking the strength even to breathe.

John finally said something like, "The doctor said that once they remove the breathing tube, Mom has only one to four hours to live."

I responded, "But what if she keeps breathing on her own?"

They sighed a sigh I will never forget. Joyce turned to look at my brothers. John elaborated and explained what the surgeon found during the surgery. We already knew she had diverticulitis with infection, which was treatable. However, as the doctor prepared to surgically treat the diverticulitis, he discovered that part of her intestines had died from a lack of blood flow. Perforations resulting from both these issues had leaked poisons throughout her system, a fatal condition.

I was stunned by their report. This was not the happy, cheer-me-up phone call I had so eagerly expected.

Tears flooded my eyes as they continued to talk. They told me that when Mom awoke from the anesthesia, she began to pull at her oxygen tube. The doctor explained to Mom that she would breathe and sleep better with it in place. My siblings added that Mom was unaware of the tragic findings during her surgery.

My head was spinning, thinking, "Is this really happening…or is this a really bad dream?"

They continued to share the news I had to hear. With the family gathered around her, the doctor had planned to tell Mom about her terminal prognosis in the morning. My siblings made a tender suggestion that I could connect via Skype in the morning (California time) when the doctor came.

As they shared this heartbreaking news, I glanced at my husband. He had a look on his face that I had never seen before. His face lost all expression, he was completely speechless; I watched his heart sinking. He loved my mother, and my mother loved him. Hearing that my precious mother was going to pass away so suddenly and knowing there was no way for me to be with her broke his heart. He knew I had to stay by his side; there was nothing he could do about it. When I saw his face lose all expression and then slowly turn away, I knew I would have to be very careful and avoid discussing my mother in front of him. I also knew this was not simply a really bad dream.

After the call, I started to cry. Thankfully, for Darrell's sake, my tears were short lived. I quickly sent an email and Facebook update, sharing my family's heartbreaking news. I asked my friends to pray for my family and for Darrell to recover quickly so we could hurry home for the funeral. I also asked God for grace. I would need much grace being so far from her, unable to say goodbye to her properly in person.

I wondered, "How am I going to make that phone call—after yearning for days to talk to her?" Saying goodbye via computer felt more than surreal; it felt terribly wrong.

Imagining I was with her…I would tell her so much. Taking her by the hand, I would tell her how much I love her, how thankful I am for all she did for me, and how important she made me feel when we came home to visit. I would tell her what a loving grandma she was to our boys and thank her for the wonderful way she treated my husband. I would share how I enjoyed talking politics with her and that I loved our fun post-race (NASCAR®) chats. How I relished making her laugh with the prank-calls I made to her at work. I would look into her eyes and tell her again and again how much I love her. Finally, if I could muster up the courage, I would finish by saying, "I dread how empty my life will be without you." I simply imagined being there at her side.

Looking at my computer screen, I began to read the expressions of love which were being lavished upon me. It was comforting, which brought me to tears, but a different kind of tears. These were tears from a thankful heart for the beautiful, caring people in my life. Suddenly, I felt a wave of peace flow over me that mere words cannot describe. It was amazing.

Drying my eyes, I stood up and began to focus on my husband who truly needed me. I knew I had to be strong for the people in Eden—the very people to whom we came to minister. Though heartbroken, I knew if I fell apart, they would think my God was inadequate to help me. I began to sing the hymn, "It Is Well" in my mind over and over.

While standing by Darrell's side, I was comforted knowing that my mom would have no doubt of my love for her. We had a wonderful and loving relationship. Though many miles separated us after I married Darrell in 1981, I phoned Mom regularly and made many trips to California to see her. During our 23 years with the Air Force and eight years in Florida after Darrell's retirement, Mom visited us several times and in several places. On countless phone calls, we recalled fond times in various cities, reminding each other of hilarious moments. My heart was warmed with these precious memories.

With Mom having only a few hours to live, I ran to the nurses' station to get the hospital's direct phone number to our room. I wanted our family members to be able to reach us immediately if necessary, especially since we had sketchy Internet service.

At this point, whenever I had to leave our room, I would pray for strength to be calm: I wanted to be a good testimony for those who worked at the hospital. I would tell myself, "Smile, Joanie, you have hope. Be strong; these precious people need to see that your God is strong." When my heart was at its heaviest, I would say with every step I took, "You have hope."

Wayne and Louise had loaned us one of their cell phones so we could contact one another. When they called to check on us, they were shocked at the update on my mom. While on their way to the hospital, they asked if there was anything I wanted. After thinking for a brief moment, there was something I really wanted: McDonald's French fries. Kind of silly and not so healthy, it was my favorite comfort food. When I am particularly sad, my husband simply pulls into the drive-thru, no need to even ask. Not long after that phone call, Louise walked in with a heartfelt hug and a large order of French fries, my "McTherapy." Thanking her, I raced into the hallway to eat them so Darrell would not be tormented by their aroma.

Wayne and Louise were so kind to us. We had come to help them and their church; instead, they were taking care of two missionaries who were wounded in very different ways. Darrell and I have said many times that they could very well have been angels. Teasing, I actually peeked under Louise's hair to check for wings. During the most difficult days in my life, they were kind beyond measure; and quite possibly, those may have been the best fries I had ever eaten.

I had to talk to our sons again, to share the regretful news. My heart ached to have to tell them they would have to Skype their beloved Grandma Carol—to say goodbye.

As the day grew more difficult, a quick trip to the balcony to take a deep breath and say a prayer refreshed my spirit.

Upon returning to Darrell's side, I was concerned that the "cleaning surgery" was not working. I desperately searched for any sign of improvement, but Darrell appeared to be even quieter than he was before. Although the news of my mom's impending death contributed to his sadness, he looked more sick than sad. The nurses continued to take Darrell's BP, temperature, and blood samples regularly. The doctor made another slow, strolling visit, but he did not seem concerned with the recent updates in Darrell's medical chart or his patient's quiet demeanor. After watching the doctor's calm manner, I trusted that Darrell's vital signs were not regressing.

CHAPTER ELEVEN

The Hardest Call of My Life

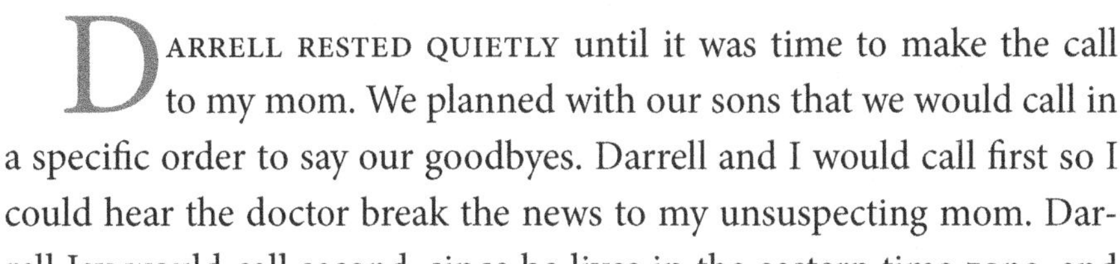

Darrell rested quietly until it was time to make the call to my mom. We planned with our sons that we would call in a specific order to say our goodbyes. Darrell and I would call first so I could hear the doctor break the news to my unsuspecting mom. Darrell Jay would call second, since he lives in the eastern time zone, and Bobby, who lives in the central time zone, would call her last.

When the dreadful time had come, my family answered my call, using my niece, Katie's laptop. The call was surprisingly clear. The laptop was placed in the next room while they waited for the doctor, who was running late. Despite our somber moods, I exchanged hellos with my family members, and it was almost therapeutic to see their faces. My niece, Elise, who had recently received her nursing degree, asked a few medical questions regarding Darrell's condition. I longed to share my fears about Darrell's doctor, but I knew it was best I did not. I did not know about a partially communist country's Internet security and their ability to eavesdrop, so I determined to be extremely careful what I said.

Once Mom's doctor arrived, the laptop was brought into her hospital room. The doctor began by discussing the surgery that happened the day before and about Mom's previous tests. I remember that he spoke above us, so to speak, using medical terms that are not a part of most people's regular vocabulary. He seemed to go on and on. Finally, he said, "I said all that to say this…" and the connection went dead. There was no sound, no picture—nothing. Just silence at the part that

I wanted to hear the most. In shock, I exclaimed, "What happened!? Where did they go?! No! Not now!" The timing was completely devastating.

Frantically, I tried to think of ways to tell my family what had happened. I was pretty certain their phones had been turned off for such an important meeting; but I tried anyway. I called every family member's cell phone number that I had, using all the money that was on my Skype account, but sadly, nobody had their phone turned on.

Finally, someone noticed the laptop's battery had died, so they sent my nephew, Daniel, to get his laptop from his car in the parking lot. At last, I received another call from my family, but when I answered, the poor connection provided a terrible audio and video transmission… and the doctor was gone. I still do not know what the doctor said or how my mom and family reacted to it. Because I live 3,000 miles from my family, I have only been to California for short, emotional visits since mom passed away, and I felt it was not the time to ask such personal questions.

The second connection was so blurry that I could only distinguish a few of my own family members. Frantic, I wrote a Skype message that the sound and video quality was bad, hoping Daniel would check the settings on his computer. Apparently, nobody had seen my note, and I briefly considered disconnecting to try for a better connection; however, because of the intermittent Internet service at the hospital, I decided to keep the call I had.

Someone angled the camera so I could see my mom, and I was stunned—first with shock and then disbelief. I had not seen Mom in person since her weight loss, so between the blurry picture and the oxygen mask she was wearing, the person I was seeing did not look like Mom. I leaned in, close to the computer, bewildered. The room was silent, except for the beeping of the machines that were keeping her alive. In the deafening silence, I realized the time had come for me to talk to my mother. Someone brought the camera close to Mom so

I could see her better... Everything was surreal—like a dream, a very bad dream.

How do you tell your mom you love her when you can hardly tell it is her? How do you say, "Goodbye," while being very careful to avoid that word? How do you express the feelings in your heart with an audience listening to your every word? The situation was more than awkward; I felt vulnerable and, in a way, embarrassed by that vulnerability.

I suddenly had a question, but with the silent room of onlookers, I dared not ask. I wanted to ask, "Did anyone else say goodbye, or am I the first one?" Because I missed the doctor's explanation, I did not know what had been said. I wanted to know if Mom understood everything. However, in a quiet room, I could not ask these questions in front of my mother. As I said once, and it bears repeating, it was both awkward and difficult—difficult to avoid telling her how sick Darrell was, difficult to avoid telling her how afraid I had been, and difficult to avoid telling her how badly I longed to be held by her. I knew it was best that she did not know about our situation. I also knew if I had started down that emotional path, I would have crumbled like a dried-up leaf.

During our frightening days with Darrell in the hospital, there was nobody on earth I wanted to speak to more than my mom. Instead of finally getting to talk to her, I was losing her. Earlier that day, in my mind, the words had easily flowed from my heart. I had envisioned a more private conversation with my mother, but now I realized that an intimate, beautiful conversation could not be a reality in this situation.

I took a deep breath, and I told my mom that I loved her very much. I told her I was sorry she was sick and that I was praying for her. Afraid I would say the wrong thing, my words did not flow as planned. There was no time to rehearse, and there were no do-overs.

As I spoke, the thin woman I saw wearing an oxygen mask could not open her eyes. My mom had such beautiful, smiling blue eyes, and if she had been able to open them, I would have instantaneously recognized her. I like to think that she was trying to open them, and I like to think that she knew it was me on the computer talking to her. My prayer is that Mom heard everything I shared and that she knew how much I loved her—even if my words failed me that day.

When it was Darrell's turn to talk, we disguised the fact he was in a hospital bed in case Mom opened her eyes. She did not need to know he was in the hospital. Darrell spoke and said many of the same things that I did. He told me later how careful he was to avoid saying "goodbye." He did not want to sound as if this would be the last time we would speak to her—even though we both knew it probably was. And it was.

I sat in the corner of the room with the computer and continued to watch and listen. Darrell had fallen asleep, but I could not pry myself from the computer. I could see that one of my sisters was stroking Mom's hair, but because of the poor connection and our close family resemblance, I could not be certain which sister it was. My sisters took turns sitting with Mom, getting very close and talking to her. How I longed to hear those sweet words of love! Instead, I could only hear the haunting sound of the breathing machine.

As I watched my sisters stroke Mom's hair, my heart felt as if it were being rent in two. I was sincerely grateful that Mom had so much love and comfort during her last moments on earth. However, I desperately longed to be there to talk to her and to stroke her hair. I shudder when I think about Mom's anticipation as she was about to go into surgery thinking the doctor would "fix her" and instead, being told she would have less than four hours to live after her machine was turned off. "Was she scared?" I wondered. "Was she in pain? Could she express her feelings?" I had a host of questions. I never felt so far away—ever.

All of a sudden, everyone gathered close to Mom. I was unable to hear anything they said, except for mentioning two random colors. "Colors? What could they be talking about?" As much as I wanted to watch every minute of my family with mom, it was rather late. I was physically and emotionally drained and I could not understand most of the things being said, anyway. I quietly ended the Skype call while they were busy discussing something with Mom.

I learned six months later Mom was trying to tell them what she wanted to wear to her own funeral. I cannot imagine how hard that must have been for everyone that day. They told me she could no longer speak but using every bit of her strength through her hand signs, their guessing, and her nodding, they learned she had chosen a green dress that was hanging in her closet.

After quietly getting ready to sleep, I moved my bedding to the sofa to be closer to Darrell's hospital bed. I had not noticed any improvement in his health—now a full 28 hours since the surgery. The reality was that he was beginning to get sicker. I could tell.

That night I felt so very alone. Even though I absolutely felt the love of God in my heart, I still longed for a hug—a good, long hug. Thoughts haunted me like, "I can't see my children, and I am unable to hug and comfort my hurting siblings," and "There are no close friends to drop by the hospital for a visit and give me that much needed hug…" My husband was right next to me, but he was asleep. Even if he awoke, he was not able to hold me in my grief—he was simply too sick.

Thankfully, God's Word came to mind. God has promised us that He will not leave us comfortless. As I remembered many verses, I felt God's peace and comfort well-up within me. I discovered that the Psalms are like a balm to a wounded heart, and He hears us when we pray. Many verses came to life in my heart that night. We really can rest in His promises, and when everything looked hopeless, I felt hope. Without a doubt, I felt the prayers of our friends and family. It was amazing! After praying one more time for my mom, my husband, and my family, I offered my sincere thanks to God for helping me once again, when I so desperately needed it.

CHAPTER TWELVE

A Spot of Tea

After such an emotional night, our daily 5:30 a.m. chant with the subsequent bird-revolt seemed to come even earlier than normal. As tired as I was, there was something I was looking forward to—by way of a cup.

Every morning we were greeted with tea service. Not only did the servers smile politely with their adorable nods of affirmation, but the tea had an amazing flavor. Darrell had raved about the tea in that part of the world for years, and he was spot-on. Never having been a tea drinker, I changed my thoughts on the alternative morning beverage after tasting this tea. It became my liquid sunshine—something to which I looked forward to during our difficult and emotional days.

The morning after saying goodbye to my mother, I longed for a cup of that tea; I even peered into the hallway until I saw them coming. With a cup in my hand, I quietly sat down at the table. As I sipped the tea, I looked at the clock and wondered if my mom was still alive.

Because Darrell looked so ill, I did not want to bring up the concerns I had regarding my mom. I found myself checking online often for the words—the words that I truly *did not* want to read.

On that particular day, the tea seemed to be extra-delicious, and in a strange way, comforting. Between my searches for news on my mother, I watched Darrell closely in case his condition should seem to improve. If so, I would ask the doctor for a projected discharge date. Then we could purchase airline tickets for our journey home for the funeral. *Home*—what a lovely word!

Finally, my computer had an update from home. Time froze as I read a tender message from my brother, Jim. He shared with me that Mom was taken off life support and was sleeping peacefully. Three of my siblings were still with her, giving her love and affection. He expressed how their day, for the most part, was "magical" and full of love. He shared how one of my mom's dear childhood friends came to visit, which meant so much to her. My heart loved hearing that, but then it quickly began to race, knowing her short span of time left on this earth had officially begun. I tried to avoid looking for messages so often, but I could not help myself. I would watch Darrell, then watch the clock, watch Darrell, and then watch the clock.

To keep my emotions under control, I slipped outside onto the balcony. I asked God for a special sign of love. I knew He would show me something special because I *really* needed it. My eyes scanned the sky and trees intently looking for "it." Soon, I spied a bright, almost fluorescent, "yellow birdie" (one of the pet names Darrell gave me.) zoom by the balcony. Wow! I told God, "Oh, that's good; but that's not it." I continued to search the entire balcony view, wondering what He would show me. On the same flight path as the yellow bird came a beautiful green parrot with a very bright red head. Red happens to be one of my (and my mom's!) favorite colors, primarily because of a particular San Francisco football team. I smiled really big and said to God, "Oh, that's good, too! But… that's still not it." With all I was going through, I needed a very special "Joanie sign!" I really did appreciate the first two birds, but I knew they were not "my" special sign for that very trying day.

Suddenly my eye caught sight of a black crow flying toward me. My first thought was, "A crow? Nah." It would not be a crow after those two beautiful birds! Then I thought I saw something in his beak. Though I kept staring at the bird, I could not tell what it was carrying. It was amazing that he was not flying to the tenth floor, and he was not flying to the eighth floor; rather, he was coming directly toward me as

I stood on my ninth-floor balcony. When the crow was just a few yards in front of me, he was close enough that I could clearly see he had a FRENCH FRY in his beak! Then he veered left to the next balcony.

Tears of joy ran down my face, and I thanked God repeatedly for being so real and personal to me. He loved me enough to bring me my favorite comfort food on such a difficult day. Somebody in Eden was sad to lose a French fry that day, but I truly needed it more.

Elated, I hurried in to tell Darrell my amazing experience. I could "kind of" tell he was happy for me, but he said nothing. My enthusiasm made up for his lack of emotion.

Consumed with the desire to get home, I asked a friend in the States to contact Delta Airlines to see if they would exchange our original tickets from Bangkok to the States for an earlier flight from Eden. I was confident that because of my husband's surgery and the imminent death of my mother, the airlines would work with us to get us home for the funeral. However, the Delta representative told them that the entire month of August was overbooked, and it would be very difficult, if not impossible, to get us on another flight. Disappointed, I planned to call Delta Airlines and our United States embassy myself, when I could. I would call anyone if it meant we could get an earlier flight. I simply wanted to go home.

CHAPTER THIRTEEN

Heartbroken and So Far from Home

THE DOCTOR WAS battling Darrell's peritonitis and ruptured colon with antibiotics and a saline wash; and I anxiously watched for any sign of improvement. Much to our dismay, we were seeing no improvement at all. In fact, he looked worse than he did the day before. Cautiously wondering if the antibiotics were enough, I continued praying for Darrell and thinking of my family.

The room's faulty air conditioning began to bother Darrell even more with its continuous shift between Arctic cold and equatorial hot. As I got up to turn it on and off when necessary, it was a welcome distraction.

With each peek at the clock, I wondered, "Is Mom comfortable, is she scared? Is she still with us?" The thought of her being afraid made me shudder. My heart's constant prayer was, "Please, dear Lord, keep her spirit calm. And please, please, let her not be in pain."

As Darrell grew even less talkative, I often stood by his side. In fact, my standing at his bedside is Darrell's most vivid memory of his stay at the hospital. I would occasionally rub Darrell's arm and lightly stroke his face, which brought back the bittersweet memory of my sisters stroking Mom's hair the night before. My longing to be with her was beyond words, it caused a lump in my throat, making it very difficult to swallow.

Reflecting on that loving action by my sisters, it suddenly brought some happy memories and actually made me laugh out loud. My thoughts went back to the time I flew to California to help Mom after her hip replacement surgery. "Nurse Joanie" happens to sleepwalk and sleep talk. The first night I slept with Mom in her bed, she started to snore. I mean no disrespect whatsoever, but Mom could snore with the best of them.

She told me that in the middle of the night, I made a loud and frustrated sigh, sat up, took my pillow, and walked to the bedroom on the other side of the house. Mom gingerly got out of bed to check on me...when I was the one who was supposed to be taking care of her! By the time she hobbled to the other bedroom, I was fast asleep! Mom and I have laughed over that fiasco countless times. I was relieved that the burst of laughter from that memory did not wake up my sleeping husband.

While watching Darrell as he rested, I closed my eyes and visualized my sisters stroking Mom's hair. I began to stroke Darrell's hair and imagined the next stroke was for my mom. Then back and forth, I took turns—a stroke for Darrell, a stroke for my mom, a stroke for Darrell and a stroke for my mom. Tears streamed silently down my face, and my resting husband had no idea of the emotional impact that had on his grieving wife.

Very concerned over the signs of Darrell's regressing heath, I had his permission to call Wayne and see if he would gather some men to anoint Darrell with oil and to pray. We strongly believe in that Biblical teaching, especially after experiencing its benefits firsthand with our son's head injury. Darrell Jay had suffered a concussion which left him with frequent migraines that nothing could relieve. After being anointed, the migraines were a rare occurrence. I also recall that anointing oil and prayer brought children after years of infertility into the lives of two families we know.

Later that morning, four Godly men surrounded my dear husband. I was thankful for the peace that the time of prayer brought to the both of us, knowing Darrell's deteriorating condition was taken before the throne of God. I was also comforted to read online that many others were praying for him as well.

Shortly after they were finished, my brother Jim sent the dreaded message: our sweet mom was no longer with us but had most gently and peacefully passed. Taking a deep breath, I turned to those in the room and simply said, "She's gone." As my eyes began to fill with tears, I thought, "While Darrell lies here so ill in a third-world-country, did I really just lose my mom…my precious mom?"

Taking another deep breath, I muffled my tears and asked God to help me be strong for Darrell's sake. One more deep breath, I turned to the computer to notify my family and friends that Mom had entered the glories of heaven. Soon, one tender comment after another appeared from the hearts of the sweet, loving people who had seen my sad update. Somehow, reading their condolences removed my buffer of unbelief, and her absence was suddenly very much a reality. The tears began to pour down my face as I grieved the loss of the mother I loved so much.

At that precise moment, during one of the hardest times of my entire life, I felt exceedingly comforted by God. It was truly amazing. Blanketed by an indescribable wave of grace, one I could literally feel. It was almost like being hit by a wave in the ocean. I was able to stand up and wipe away my tears. I was awed and humbled by God's gift of a calm, peaceful heart…and so thankful that He would reach down and help me in my time of desperate need.

I immediately began to sing within my soul, and then later dwell on two songs, "It Is Well With My Soul" and "What a Day That Will Be." Music is powerful, and both of these songs burst with a message of hope. I took a short break and walked onto the balcony, thanking God as I marveled at the calm I was feeling. Walking back into the room, I could see my husband had a new look about him, and it was *not* good.

After the passing of my mother, I did not need to check the computer for updates about her condition any longer. The timing was good because I needed to focus all of my attention on Darrell. He began to turn a pale shade of green, and I cannot describe how unsettling it was to see this development.

Up to this point, I had been very open with my prayer warriors during our combined crises with Darrell's failing health and the death of my mother. However, I knew I had to be somewhat vague about this downward turn. I did not want our sons to read online how sick their dad was or to frighten our family members more than they already were. As much as I wanted to, I could not share that I had grave concerns and felt we would lose him.

Wayne, Tom, and I sat quietly in the room, helplessly watching Darrell decline. We would look at Darrell, then at one another. We spoke volumes without words. In my mind's eye, I can still see their expressions. I remember the tilted head and the tight-lipped grimace, with a look that said, "I am not sure he will make it." I would sigh and mirror the same look back.

The thought of losing my husband filled me with sheer, utter fright. My prayer for the rest of the day was, "Please Lord, not *both* of them at the same time." I could not imagine the grief of losing the two dearest people on earth—within mere hours of each other.

The nurses started to come in our room more frequently to take Darrell's temperature and BP, noting them in his chart. After drawing multiple vials of blood, they would label them and quietly leave the room. This pattern continued for hours, while Darrell grew more and more quiet.

Unable to share my fears, a ball of emotion began to well up inside me. Three little words would have summed up how I was feeling: ***"I'm really scared!"*** However, sharing those words would not have served any purpose but to alarm our children and family who were so far away.

The doctor came into the room with his usual slow swagger, clearly displaying his lack of urgency regarding Darrell's condition. After a brief visit, he left without giving us an update—again. The three of us were growing more and more anxious—not knowing what this doctor was waiting for or why. Did he plan to continue with this façade of care while Darrell died before our very eyes?

Some people use the phrase, "Silence is golden," but to this wife, her husband's quietness was deeply unsettling. After hours of silent rest, Darrell sat up and suddenly, and quite loudly blurted out with a stern, strong voice, "Whatever it is, take it, take it now!" while pointing to his abdomen. His outcry took my breath away! This outburst, together with the doctor's seeming lack of care for his dying patient, alarmed me. I certainly did not want *this* doctor to put my husband under general anesthesia and perform major surgery; however, the alternative was much worse.

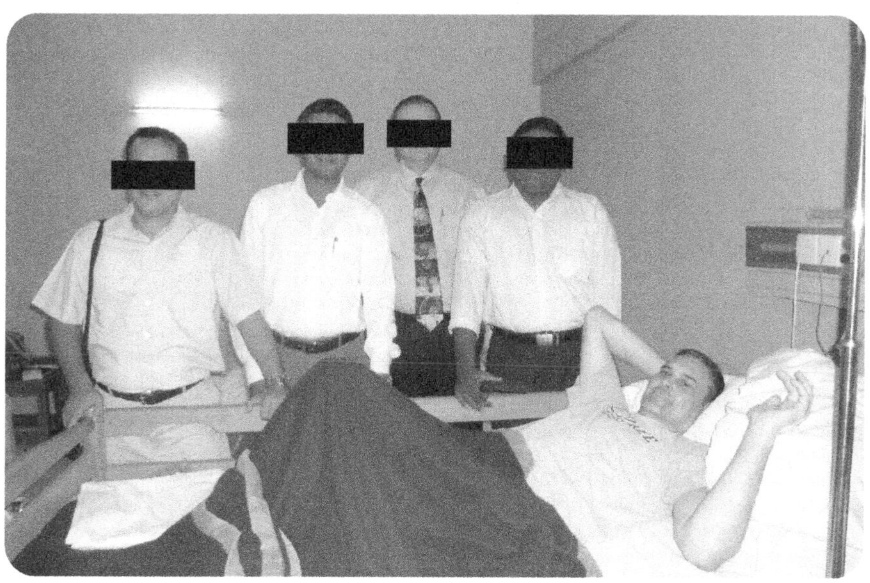

Anointing Darrel with oil before his rapid decline

Mom and me

CHAPTER FOURTEEN

"Halfway to Heaven..."

After Darrell's sudden outburst, I ran to the nurses' station to alert them that we needed the doctor to come to the room immediately. Continuing in a panicky tone, I told them that Darrell was declining quickly and had outright requested surgery. Thankfully, the doctor returned in a reasonable amount of time. He clearly sensed our fears as we tried to verbalize our frustration about the delays. I was thankful that I did not have to confront this doctor alone. Tom and new friend, Wayne, the tall, broad-shouldered missionary, were with us in the room. I remember when Wayne stood up, the doctor appeared to be somewhat intimidated.

The doctor responded to our requests and fears by saying, "I think it's time I call in a colleague."

Relieved, my only thought was, *Finally!*

After the doctor left the room, we continued with our nervous glances, hoping and praying Darrell would get to surgery in time. As we waited together in silence, an older doctor walked into our room. He was kind and had an air of medical authority. After reviewing the CAT scan results and pictures of Darrell's peritonitis taken two days earlier, he exclaimed that both the white blood count and fever had spiked, followed with an emphatic, "Surgery needs to be done today!" He continued explaining that he would remove the ruptured segment of colon and perform the Hartmann's procedure. This surgery entails diverting Darrell's intestines to a colostomy bag, which would collect the fecal matter from his body. Calmly, our new doctor sketched a drawing of what he planned to do, while giving us a crash-course on the necessary, life-saving surgery. Then, assuring us he would be back that afternoon, he handed me his business card and walked out the door.

We looked at each other, stunned! We did not think it was possible that a five-minute encounter could take us from great fear of surgery to great peace. What a huge answer to prayer! Wayne looked at the business card and told us his title indicated that he was the best surgeon in this field—in the entire country! Wow! God not only replaced the doctor who had delayed Darrell's medical treatment, but He had replaced him with the best doctor available! It was such a relief to feel the load of emotional weight come off my shoulders.

The first doctor came back into the room, requesting that Darrell have another CAT scan. Not knowing at that time how horrific the first one had been for him, I was surprised when Darrell immediately said, "No!" His refusal to have the CAT scan made me question, "Could Darrell be too ill to make proper medical decisions?" Thankfully, I did not press him for the second scan. The doctor then suggested an ultrasound, and Darrell agreed. I decided to go along this time since Darrell was getting weaker, and to be honest, greener.

When we entered the elevator to go downstairs for the ultrasound, a local woman was already on the elevator, and she startled me by asking why we were in the hospital. Not expecting such a forward question, I was surprised that I actually answered her. I told her that my husband's colon had ruptured, and he needed more surgery and would soon have a colostomy bag.

Smiling back, and in a very calm manner she said to me, "My son had that surgery, and everything went well. Your husband will be fine."

The lady exited the elevator on the next floor, and the doors closed. I was amazed that we were able to have that verbal exchange on a less than one-minute elevator ride! Overwhelmed with peace, I wondered, "Could I have just met an angel?" Tears welled in my eyes as I thought on the absolutely perfect timing of such a brief encounter.

Reaching the main level of the hospital, I waited while the nurse rolled Darrell into the procedure room for the ultrasound. Too restless to sit, I stood thinking about and praying for Darrell. Suddenly, I noticed another fair-skinned couple! Excited to greet them, I learned that not only were they fellow Americans, but that they were also Christians ministering in the area! What a comfort to talk to them while the ultrasound was performed on Darrell! The couple assured me they would pray for Darrell and his impending surgery.

Amazed at the two such encounters—the lady in the elevator and the sweet Christian couple—I breathed a sincere prayer, "Thank You, God, for being *so good* to me." When the procedure was over, the nurse took Darrell back to our room, where he quietly waited for surgery.

As the nurses continued the frequent temperature and BP checks, I asked one of the nurses if Darrell's fever had gone up. Lifting the cover paper to see the graph, she answered, "Yes.", before leaving the room. I caught a glimpse of the graph, and every new mark she had made indicated his fever was higher than the previous check. She also made a line going through all the marks. I never asked how high his temperature got, but upon seeing the line, I could tell his fever went up at an alarming rate.

Suddenly, Darrell told me that he was having difficulty breathing and that his chest was getting heavy. Taking slow, deep breaths to contain my panic, I began to rub his arm. Fear gripped me, and I began to question in my mind, "Could the long delay by the first doctor be causing my husband unnecessary pain?" Then with added horror, I thought, "Could the pain in his chest mean it's too late?"

I knew at that moment what "stark fear" felt like. I suppressed my fears to avoid revealing my grave concerns to my family, friends, and most importantly, Darrell. I knew as I took this new burden to God that I had to trust Him to take care of both Darrell's physical needs and my emotional needs.

Soon after posting a prayer request for the upcoming, complex surgery, we were inundated with replies from our precious family and friends. I read every comment, email, and all the Bible verses quoted. I carefully read every prayer and song which people took the time to write out. I read each of the prayers aloud to Darrell before he went to surgery. I even gave Darrell kisses "sent" by loved ones. As much as I wanted to read each comment to him before surgery, I could not. First, he was too weak. Second, there were simply too many! Instead, I read him the name of every person that was praying for him. His only response was a brief smile and a weak nod.

We can never express what it meant to see the many comments written on our behalf. Those words were a balm to my heart, and they provided me much needed strength; they served as the virtual hugs I needed so badly. (Since returning to the States, I have read every email and comment made during our two-month trip—multiple times. I always feel blessed and reading them often makes me weep. I am always touched to see the outpouring of love from so many compassionate people.)

While waiting for the surgery, our room became quite busy. The nurses continued to stream in and out, while the office personnel began the paperwork for the surgery. One lady from admissions told me that while Darrell would spend a few days in the intensive care unit (ICU), I could continue to stay in the hospital. However, I would have to pay $200 a night to do so. Wayne, without hesitation, said I could stay in their guest room. His kind gesture meant more to me than simply saving money. With the recent events with my mom and Darrell, I needed the encouragement I knew I would receive from their company. While I was signing a stack of surgical authorization papers, someone from the billing department handed me the bill for **all** the charges we had incurred to this point. Stamped on the top was a *cheerful* "To be paid within 24 hours." I can still recall the clicking her shoes made while she walked up to me that day.

I was disheartened to see their concern for payment, while I had concern if I would still have a husband. What an extremely emotional moment that was for me. I had succeeded thus far in repressing the emotions of losing my mom and possibly losing my husband. However, I was suddenly aware that I was also responsible for the enormous hospital bill that had been handed to me.

The bill was detailed and many pages long. Everything was listed: the items used in the first surgery, the anesthesiologist fees, the CAT scan, the medicines, the ultrasound, all of my meals, the IV bags, the laundry from his bedding, the cotton balls from the shots, the toilet paper in our room—the itemization went on and on. If anything had been used during Darrell's stay up to this point, it was included in the bill. The lady from the billing office made it very clear that the bill would need to be paid in full before his second surgery.

Wayne kindly escorted me to the bottom level of the hospital to the cashier's cage, where I handed over my credit card. As she was converting the hospital bill into U.S. dollars, I spied a sign that caused me additional alarm. "All surgeon fees must be paid in cash before patient release." Darrell and I had brought cash on the trip—but not that kind of cash!

Upon my return to the room, I received an email from dear friends from our Air Force days. In an urgent manner, they told me to take Darrell to another country as quickly as possible, adding a link for an air ambulance. At this point, Darrell was about to go into surgery, and I could not make the proper arrangements without a phone. Aside from the communication issue, Darrell was declining too fast to delay his surgery for anything. I reluctantly had to let that option go.

Meanwhile, Darrell lay green with peritonitis. The wretched smell from the poisons spreading within his body began to pour out in his breath. Although his body was dying, his spirit was in an amazingly wonderful place. Darrell later shared that he was in another realm—a realm with no time. I have heard other near-death experiences described in the same manner—a place with no time. It was not that a clock on the wall was missing; rather, there was the knowledge that time did not exist in this "special" place.

Darrell could not tell how long he was actually in this place—maybe a few minutes or as long as a few hours. He explained that he was surrounded by brightness, but there was no source of the light. Neither were there any shadows, and the level of brightness was the same throughout the entire realm. He shared that he felt as though he was floating or weightless and in a very relaxed position. He said, "You know, when you are about to go to sleep, and you get into a very comfortable position right before drifting off. That is what it was like, but I was more upright."

While Darrell was in the realm, he had no pain whatsoever, and he was in complete peace. He called it, "Perfect peace." He continued, "I felt like I was halfway to Heaven, and that I was personally in the security of God's own hand." Darrell had no fear—only total comfort.

He thought to himself, "If I were to die, it would be okay because this is so nice."

Interestingly, Darrell began to describe how he experienced love in multiple dimensions. He felt love in his heart but also the "warmth of love" throughout his whole body. He likened it to a baby's feeling of comfort while being wrapped in his parent's loving arms—complete, pure, and perfect love. When asked if he had seen any loved ones who had passed on before him, Darrell simply responded, "No." However, he quickly added, "The warmth of love that I felt could be compared to the feeling you get when gathered with loved ones at a joyous occasion."

Over a year had passed before Darrell began to share this near-death experience—even with me. He waited that long simply because he lacked words to adequately describe what had happened.

As he finished recounting this marvel, tears rolled down my face. Hearing what he told me made my heart feel very secure in my faith and in the reality of Heaven. I asked, "Do you know how rare this is and how special you are to have experienced this?!"

He looked at me and quietly answered, "Yes."

CHAPTER FIFTEEN

Surgery #2, On Demand!

Surgery is something most people avoid and even something to dread—until this day. I was beyond relieved when the nurse came to take Darrell to the OR. My short, but continual prayers changed often that particular day, until I finally begged, "Please Lord, let it not be too late!"

During his surgery, I experienced a cruel phenomenon—time appeared to move in slow motion, although that is probably to be expected while waiting for something of this magnitude. I longed to hear the doctor say, "Your husband will be just fine."

Tom, Wayne, and Louise left for church services that evening, and a kind lady offered to sit in my room so I wasn't alone. In the quietness, I reflected on the day's events. I grabbed my computer—my lifeline to loved ones—as a child would grab for their favorite blanket. While absorbed in reading notes from family and friends, I was surprised to see messages from strangers. With my husband in life-saving surgery and despite the loss of my mom, I had a peaceful heart. I attribute that peace to the many prayers offered on our behalf, it was truly a gift from God.

The more I read, the more I saw the same heartfelt sentiment—people assuring us of their prayers. Our dear friend, Sharon, wrote, "I should be asleep but want to stay here and 'hold your hand.'"

I find it impossible to convey the peace I felt and deep gratitude for those expressions of love from our family and friends. While reading their priceless words, tears of thankfulness filled my eyes, causing their writing to blur. Unable to read for my overflowing emotion, I would stop to pray. I continued to read and pray until the nurse came to tell me the surgery was over. I could finally go to the OR.

Making my way up the stairs, I searched for ways to mentally prepare myself, in case the surgeon brought me the worst possible news. I immediately thought of the Bible story of Job when all of his children had been killed. He said, *"...the LORD gave, and the Lord hath taken away; blessed be the name of the LORD"* (Job 1:21). I repeated those words slowly in my mind.

As I sat outside the OR, waiting for the surgeon was agonizing, especially not knowing the outcome of the surgery. I often prayed, "Please, Lord, let him be fine. Please, Lord." I reminded God that we were there to help people and to tell them about His Son, Jesus; I asked Him to have mercy on Darrell. Then suddenly, I remembered that I did not need to remind God who we were; of course, He knows everything already—even how many hairs we have on our heads.

Finally, the surgeon arrived carrying a shiny stainless-steel tray. After telling me that Darrell was stable and in recovery, he explained that he thought it was important to show me what he had removed from my husband's body. Darrell's sigmoid colon was on that tray, and it looked like something right out of a horror movie. Stunned by the severity of the sight, I was thankful that I have always been medically minded. The tray held a thick, nearly foot-long, dark red and pink specimen with splotches of red, green, and white. Grotesque bubbles of differing sizes covered the diseased colon. The doctor explained that his colon had become abscessed. As he turned it over to show me the rupture, I saw black discoloration around the hole. At that moment, I knew why Darrell was green—he had been slowly dying on the inside. The doctor told me that Darrell had sepsis,[1] and that the surgery was absolutely necessary.

The doctor continued to explain that because Darrell's surgery was quite extensive, he would need to stay in the ICU for a couple of days.

When he finished speaking with me, the doctor returned to the OR. I found it impossible to leave, so I simply sat in the waiting area, knowing my Darrell was just beyond the doors.

After church ended, Tom, Wayne, and Louise joined me in the waiting area. Once again, they brought me something therapeutic—more French fries! They were so kind, like ministering angels.

As we were visiting, I saw a nurse wheel Darrell from the OR into the ICU. In a burst of uncontrolled excitement, I shrieked emotionally, "I love you!!" To my surprise, he nodded! (Although Darrell has no recollection of my outburst, I was thrilled to see him acknowledge me.) That one-sided micro-communication with my husband truly set my heart at ease. Filled with excitement to tell everyone the good news, my next thought was to call my mom. Jolted back to reality, I realized I had been so focused on Darrell's deteriorating condition and surgery, that I had not even begun to truly grasp the loss of my mother.

As I gathered our belongings from the room, I looked forward to going back to Wayne and Louise's home. I was ready to place my exhausted body on a real bed and have peace and quiet rather than the repeated "squeak" of the BP box. Their guest room sounded like paradise!

The lessons we have learned since our return to the States have been staggering. From the time the doctor saw Darrell's ruptured colon during surgery on Monday, to the time Darrell demanded surgery Wednesday night, we inherently trusted the doctor's wisdom. After all, doctors take an oath and are supposed to help people, right? Unfortunately, that was not the case in this situation.

Darrell and I discussed adding medical definitions to this book to allow readers to understand his conditions without requiring research. We had no idea what that decision would entail. I already knew what sepsis was, and I had learned in Eden what peritonitis was, but I had no idea what a doctor should and should not do when a colon ruptures. I researched medical websites to understand better the proper treatment for Darrell's illness. As I read the information, I began to weep.

First, let me share the facts: Perforation of the colon is a life-threatening condition, and the patient needs to undergo surgery **as soon as possible**. The danger of a colon rupture is connected to fecal leakage into the peritoneum. Bacteria and their toxins can affect the internal organs, become further absorbed and get into the bloodstream. This can cause sepsis which can lead to a lethal outcome.

Second, I will share our reality: Monday morning during the CAT scan, the technician blasted water into Darrell's rectum through a long tube. As I have already mentioned, that procedure literally **forced** fecal matter throughout his peritoneum, ultimately causing his entire body to be affected by the poison. Having this understanding explained why close to nine hours later, the doctor exclaimed, "This is the worst care of peritonitis I have ever seen!"

The CAT scan showed Darrell had an enlarged appendix and by the time he finally had surgery on Wednesday, other organs were enlarged from the invasive poison. I also discovered that in emergency situations when diverticulitis is suspected, medical personnel are instructed not to do any procedures rectally. I had clearly informed the doctor that Darrell had twice suffered with mild diverticulitis. In addition, his first blood test on Saturday night indicated infection.

During surgery on Monday, the doctor ***saw*** Darrell's ruptured, abscessed colon and even though Darrell was already under general anesthesia, the doctor chose not to repair it. I fail to understand how he could see a life-threatening situation, ignore the solution, and tell me, "I rinsed his abdomen with saline." As I searched the Internet for answers, every website declared the same answer: a ruptured colon needs to be repaired immediately—before peritonitis sets in.

Nearly one year later after the fact, I now understand why our Air Force friends begged us to call an air ambulance and why others suggested that we go anywhere else for treatment. We absolutely trusted that the doctor was treating Darrell properly, and I was also distracted with the simultaneous death of my mother. As Darrell rapidly declined, we knew we could not remove his IV and simply drive to the airport. We did not have airline tickets, and at all times, Darrell needed intravenous antibiotics and pain medicine. What a frightening situation we were in!

While watching the doctor treat Darrell with his slow, deliberate demeanor, we were completely ignorant of the fact that Darrell was in a life-threatening situation. The other doctor who saved Darrell's life told me that if we had left that day, Darrell would have died—probably before he could ever board a plane. We are humbled and eternally grateful, knowing Darrell's survival was a gift from God—a true modern-day miracle.

> Without appropriate treatment, feculent peritonitis from a perforated colon is universally fatal. Bro. Bolton's survival despite delays in treatment testifies to the grace of God.
>
> – Christopher W. Snyder, MD Major
> USAF MC General Surgeon

> When [I was told] of Darrell's ordeal in a foreign country it brought back memories of my husband's perforated bowel hospitalization. I am a registered nurse with 48 years of hospital experience and understand the dangers of peritonitis. My husband had the benefit of an excellent surgeon, the best in nursing care and most of all sanitation. Even with all those benefits there was still a 50% chance my husband would die. The fact that Darrell lived was truly a miracle.

A miracle is not to be taken lightly because, by definition, there is no other answer except that God's divine intervention caused the healing to happen. In Darrell's case there is no other answer; God miraculously healed him for His glory.

– Jean Kilts, BSN, RN, CDE

IT IS AMAZING that Darrell lived through this treatment. While surgery was delayed four days, he had a perforated colon, allowing toxins and waste to spill into the abdominal cavity, causing peritonitis. Without treatment, peritonitis can rapidly spread into the blood causing sepsis, organ failure and death. Post-surgical patients with peritonitis need close, close monitoring for possible infection and wound healing complications. Why he didn't experience organ failure due to the delay of surgery is a miracle.

- Cynthia Huntley, RN

AS A NURSE of over 25 years, I have encountered many patients in a variety of conditions. Meeting Darrell is truly nothing short of a miracle because Darrell shouldn't even be here. Let me make this clear: Darrell had many complications which should have taken his life, but through the grace of God and the care and aggressive advocacy of his wife, he survived. God had a different plan. He allowed Darrell not only to recover, but flourish.

– Donna Nagel, RN, MSN

---

[1] *Sepsis:* a life-threatening complication of an infection. To improve the chance of survival, early treatment requires high dose antibiotics and large amounts of intravenous fluids.

CHAPTER SIXTEEN

ICU; Day One

While peacefully drinking my coffee at our host's home, I noticed the gentle morning rain and a playful return of the monkeys. What a wonderful way to start my day! I relished my first night without nurse interruptions, and I was relieved to know Darrell was under the constant care of trained nurses in the ICU and would be closely monitored throughout the night.

My peaceful morning was short lived when I received a mass email announcement with my mom's date of birth and date of death as the subject line. My heart began to beat faster as I opened the email and read the words. My heart immediately sank as I realized that I would miss my own mother's funeral. I wish I could say I handled that news better; however, a loud, pain-filled cry escaped my lips. Wayne and Louise immediately rushed from their bedroom to check on me. I explained what I had just read and assured them I would be fine.

Somehow Darrell and I had hoped that Mom's funeral could be delayed until we were home. At that moment, I was emotionally unprepared to learn that the funeral could not be postponed. I immediately began to pray, asking God for the emotional and physical strength I would need with having learned this news. I quickly made a post on Facebook asking for prayer with the disappointing update.

In His love, He answered almost before I finished! I was deeply thankful, because I knew that when I went to the hospital to see Darrell, I needed to be happy and positive.

Shortly after breakfast, Louise took me to the ICU to see Darrell.

Visitors were only allowed two times a day, and for only fifteen minutes. That was fine because I knew Darrell required rest after all his body had endured. As we pulled into the hospital's parking garage, we came to a ticket booth. I was overwhelmed when I realized Wayne and Louise had to pay each time they came to visit us, which was often multiple times a day! They were always exceedingly cheerful and supportive; I never imagined their visits required payment. Words fail to explain how special this family is to us.

Upon reaching the ICU, we were greeted by a sign which instructed us to take off our shoes and step into a pair of community, plastic, clog-like shoes, which were lined up on a rack. I was surprised at this health-related policy, considering the unsanitary conditions I had already seen.

Even more shocking to see was the doctor's personal lack of sanitation. The first doctor checked Darrell's wounds with unwashed hands, and he never once used gloves. The rules seemed incredibly inconsistent. Nevertheless, I reluctantly obeyed the sign and walked in to see my honey, inwardly cringing at the thought of wearing someone else's shoes (germs!).

The ICU was a fairly small room, and the beds were very close to each other. I did not pay attention to the other patients, knowing my time with Darrell was so short. I was thrilled to finally see him, after such a complex surgery.

My first reaction was one of shock, upon seeing my once strong husband wearing an oxygen mask for the first time. Darrell was very weak, but he seemed to be calm in spirit. He now had a port in his neck so the nurse could quickly administer medicine if needed. Everything looked so scary, yet I tried not to let those feelings show. His voice was like music to my ears, though his words were few. After giving us some time alone, Louise also stepped into a pair of plastic shoes and entered the room. Darrell told us the nurses had taken great care of him, for which I was relieved. I was careful to stay for only the allotted 15 minutes; I could tell he needed the rest. Kissing him on the forehead, I told him I loved him, and that many people were praying for him.

Louise then took me to a mall to replace my luggage. The handle on my suitcase had broken on our way to Eden. Since Darrell was still able to pull it, I planned on keeping it. However, I now had a husband who required wheelchair assistance. With my lifting limitations, we needed to find something that was easy for me to maneuver. We found some interesting lightweight luggage, and each had a smooth 360° rotating wheel system. I found replacing my beautiful luggage emotionally difficult, as I vividly recalled my mom complimenting it on many of our trips to visit her. Nearly every situation that came up seemed to bring to mind another clear memory of Mom. At least this new luggage seemed like it would be perfect for two weary travelers on their long journey home. Interestingly, I overlooked a feature of the luggage: it was disposable. Yes, it was incredibly light and easy to pull and turn. However, it had fallen apart by the time we landed in Florida. Ironically, the rotating wheel system was quite helpful when I pulled it out to the curb with the trash.

After leaving the mall with the luggage, Louise offered to take me to lunch. Aside from the wonderful opportunity to relax and visit with her, it was glorious to sit somewhere other than in a hospital room. The restaurant served us an amazing pumpkin soup. Much to our delight, the chef drew happy pictures on the top of the soup with the cream. Having never experienced soup art before, I took pictures to show Darrell later. Making our way to the car, we noticed a gorgeous, fuchsia-colored flower laying on my side of the windshield. And the flower was one of my favorites—a plumeria. Also, the flower happened to match my skirt perfectly! Louise verbalized my thought—that God placed it there just for me. I took a picture of the flower by my skirt to remember the special gift I received that day.

Next, Louise took me to buy some saris and then to a seamstress to have them altered. A sari (also spelled saree) is a beautiful dress in which a very long (15 feet or more) piece of material is strategically wrapped around the body. Once wrapped and pleated, a sari is stunning with its gorgeous, flowing fashion. The sari material was reasonably priced and a good way to remember a trip that, in many ways, changed our lives forever.

When we returned to the hospital for our afternoon visit, I noticed an elderly lady in the bed next to Darrell. Louise gave her a tract while I spoke to Darrell. I noticed her staring at me with a beaming smile! She likely was surprised to see a blonde lady standing next to her. While Louise talked to Darrell, the lady reached out her hands for me. I took a step, held her fragile hands, and leaned-in to talk to her. Smiling, I told her my name and that I hoped she would feel better. She began to tell me her name; however, she started to laugh—giggling into her oxygen mask. When I started to let go, she gripped me firmly, pulling me back. I smiled and told her we came to Eden to do mission work and that I would pray for her to get better. She told me she was Buddhist; then while holding tightly to my hands, she started to laugh again. I tried one more time to let go, but she grasped me even more tightly and pulled me very close to her face. She stared into my blue eyes and began to laugh again. Smiling at her laughter, I wished her well and asked her to read the tract. When I told her I needed to speak with my husband, she released her grip. Something brought her to the ICU that day, but the sweet, giggling lady with the fragile hands was unbelievably strong!

Turning back to Darrell, I could see how weak he was. He was able to tell us that he felt fine but was tired—and added that the nurses took great care of him. After the lack of care from the first doctor, I was even more thankful for the ICU nursing staff. I made sure to thank them as I left. As much as I wanted to stay, I knew he needed rest. Even the few words he had spoken had worn him out.

When Louise and I got home, I asked to use their phone to make an important call. I needed to call Tricare, our military insurance. Since I was in Asia, the U.S. agent I spoke to could not help me, so he gave me the number to the Singapore office. When I spoke to the agent in Singapore, he informed me that our "Prime" coverage plan did not cover us when we traveled overseas. I was absolutely stunned at what the agent was telling me. He continued by explaining that on future trips, we would need to change our coverage to the "Standard" plan, where we would be fully reimbursed for medical expenses. The agent suggested that we submit the hospital bills when we got back to the U.S.; however, there was no guarantee that we would be reimbursed. Hearing this troubling financial news added a new burden to my already grieving heart. I tried to avoid thinking about the financial responsibilities we faced, but in my weariness, I did let the situation get to me a few times.

With Darrell under close medical care, I felt comfortable going to a different church that night with Wayne, Louise, and Tom. This second church was started to minister to a specific language group in Eden. Louise wrapped me in my sari for the first time, and I loved it! Services were held in an upper room which had no air conditioning, so I was extremely hot. I was asked to share my testimony that night, and a gentleman interpreted for me.

After services, a curry meal was provided. This time, however, there were no utensils! I teased Tom, "No picture taking allowed as I eat curry, rice, and gravy with my long fingernails!" What a thrill it was to spend time getting to know the people there, and especially their adorable children! I enjoyed the evening very much. The people of Eden are truly genuine and kind.

Joanie and Louise wearing their sarees

CHAPTER SEVENTEEN

ICU; Day Two

COFFEE AND WILDLIFE: what an extremely therapeutic pair! Gorgeous birds, playful monkeys, and stealth-like monitors brought a gentle diversion from the unbelievable emotional events I had experienced. I was soaking in the beauty of Eden while I lived outside the hospital for a couple of days.

When Louise took me to visit Darrell in the ICU, I noticed an older lady in a bed across from Darrell. Her arms reached upward, away from her body, but her eyes were closed. I was surprised to see that she was clearly posturing,[1] which oftentimes precedes death. I quickly turned my attention to Darrell to see how he was feeling. We had visited for only a few minutes when a nurse asked me to leave. Confused by her request, I made sure she knew I had recently arrived.

She responded to my explanation by telling me, "I'm sorry, you have to leave right now!" I walked out of the ICU and back to my street shoes, where Louise asked me what was going on. Before I could say a word, a young lady—apparently the granddaughter of the lady who was posturing—quickly came out of the ICU. Crying, she told someone on the phone, "She just passed." It was sobering to know that while Darrell and I were speaking, that elderly woman had passed away.

Later, Darrell shared several experiences while he was in the ICU. He told me the lady who was posturing had also been making the death rattle [2] many hours before I came to visit. Her labored breathing was accompanied by long, deep groans. Darrell tried his best to sleep, to avoid hearing the eerie and disquieting sounds. He remembered that in addition to her arms posturing, her knees were bent upward as well. He described her as frail...as if dark skin was lying on top of bones. When Darrell awoke from one of his naps, he watched three Buddhist monks enter the room. Clad in white robes with gold sashes, they carried drums which were strapped over their shoulders. As they gathered around the dying woman's bed, they started to play their drums. They began to chant to the rhythmic beat in their attempts to usher the woman into eternity. Unable to speak but a few words at a time, my brokenhearted husband wished he had had the strength to tell her the Gospel message of Christ.

Shortly after Darrell's second surgery, he witnessed two of his ICU nurses looking through his toiletry bag. He watched them take out his jar of hair wax and look at the label which they could not read. After taking off the lid, they both smelled it, and apparently, they liked what they smelled. Thinking it was a thick body lotion, they both proceeded to rub the hair wax all over his arms, chest, and back. Darrell was too weak to tell them to stop. What a comical story we love to share!

After being forced to leave the ICU early, Louise took me to pick up the tailored blouses for the saris and then to a mall for a chair massage. She knew I had slept on the couch in the hospital, and that I had a very stressful couple of days. How thoughtful!

As we drove through town, I noticed a man standing on a corner wearing camouflage gear, he was carrying a large automatic rifle. When we reached the next corner, we saw another man dressed the same way, also carrying a very large weapon. Corner after corner, we saw men holding guns. What a frightening way to learn of the political unrest that Eden experiences.

On our return to the hospital later that afternoon, the nurse informed me that Darrell would be released from the ICU later that night. I was relieved that Darrell had improved enough that he would no longer require constant care. However, by the time he was finally released, it was nearly midnight. I followed behind as Darrell was wheeled into our new room. I was a little disappointed as we were across the hall from the previous room, losing the beautiful view of the tree-lined park. After getting Darrell situated for the night, I made my bed on the sofa. I was once again living in a hospital room, watching after my very weak husband. I was concerned, wondering how long recovery would take after such a complex surgery.

---

[1] *Posturing*: Involuntary body movements as in the raising of arms. This can present at imminent death or as the result of brain damage.

[2] *Death rattle*: loud, laboring breathing which can preceed death

CHAPTER EIGHTEEN

Old Man Shuffle

WAKING UP THE first morning in our new room, I was grateful that the 5:30 a.m. chants were not as loud as they were on the other side of the hall. The quieter mornings were great; nevertheless, I really missed the pretty birds. I sat alone at the table drinking that wonderful tea. On occasion, I would take a sip and say to Darrell dramatically, "This tea is so good!" forgetting he was unable to eat or drink yet. Embarrassed by my lack of manners, I felt like a football player who should be penalized for unsportsmanlike conduct.

Later that morning, I was surprised when a physical therapist came to the room and asked Darrell to sit up. With curled fists pressed firmly against my mouth, I was deeply concerned with this movement after Darrell's recent complex abdominal surgery and colostomy. It took some effort, but Darrell eventually sat up. That was all the therapist had him do that day—sit up and let his feet dangle over the side of the bed. Not long after the therapist left, two nurses arrived to put post-surgical compression stockings[1] on Darrell's legs. The stockings were extremely tight but necessary to help with the prevention of clots. I felt bad as I watched the two petite nurses struggle for several minutes to get them on Darrell's long legs.

As my husband rested quietly, I pondered Mom's upcoming funeral. In my desperation to be there, I called my family via Skype to ask them to consider delaying the funeral, hoping that we would be able to travel back to California soon. (A friend had informed me the day before that funerals are often delayed. In my grief, I had desperately clung to that hope.)

In hindsight, I wish I had never made that call. I failed to take into consideration that we were all much too emotional for such a conversation, with services only days away. As much as my heart ached to be there, I knew it was best for the funeral not to be delayed. My only regret is that I put my family through such an emotional phone call. After pleading for emotional strength, God answered my prayer. I immediately felt nothing but tenderness for my siblings as they prepared for one of the most difficult days of our lives.

While the funeral itself would be formal and not appropriate for a laptop, my family suggested that they could call via Skype for me to see some of the viewing service. Doing so would also allow me to say hello to a few relatives. I was glad for the idea…it would be a tiny bit like my being there.

That afternoon we enjoyed a short, but pleasant, visit from a sweet family from Eden. The family was extremely kind with adorable children. Wayne said that many people had expressed their desire to come see us. With their hearts of gold, they simply wanted to comfort us in our trial. He told me that had he allowed them to come, quite a large crowd would have been present. He knew that Darrell needed rest more than anything, so he encouraged the would-be visitors to stay home and pray.

As we spoke to this kind family, Darrell made a statement that literally took my breath away.

"As soon as I recover enough to be cleared for travel, we will fly directly to California to attend the funeral of my wife's mother."

When I heard his statement, I quickly spun around as tears came flooding to my eyes—knowing he still believed we would be able to attend the funeral. I longed for the ability to hide my telltale emotions, but there was no mistaking something was terribly wrong with the comment Darrell had made. I knew the subject of Mom's funeral was something to avoid, as I wanted him to recover with as little emotional interference as possible.

When our company left, a respiratory therapist came to our room. He taught Darrell a breathing exercise, which would help to keep his lungs clear from fluid buildup. The therapist had Darrell blow into a breathing apparatus that had plastic balls inside. He instructed Darrell to use it multiple times a day, blowing hard until all of the little balls lifted to a particular height. Later, a different respiratory therapist came to the room; however, his job was to cup his hand and slap Darrell's back, which is another type of therapy for the lungs.

The rest of the day was spent very quietly, as I consciously pushed down the building of emotions I felt regarding Mom's death. As much as I yearned to express myself, I avoided spilling my heartbreak openly to my weak and recovering husband. As I watched Darrell as he rested, I couldn't help but notice the drainage bag which had begun to collect fluid from an abdomen once filled with poison. It was a stark reminder of how extremely ill he was.

The following day when the physical therapist returned, he asked Darrell to stand up. Albeit a little nervous, I was excited to see Darrell finally standing upright! I was delighted to see even the slightest progress. The day after, the therapist not only had him stand, but he decided Darrell would take a short five-minute walk! With a blend of excitement and fear, we had to do some pre-walk preparations. After the abdominal and catheter drainage bags were hooked to the IV pole, Darrell was finally able to leave his bed. His first few steps were so cute; I affectionately called it his "old man shuffle."

Darrell shuffled very slowly to the doorway and as he entered the hallway, he looked both ways. He chose to turn right and shuffling along, he made his way to the small nurses' desk near the end of the hallway. When he reached the desk, he tapped his hand firmly on top of it, then quickly spun around, as only socks on tile could allow! With a move reminiscent of a childhood game, the stunned nurses, therapist, and I all burst into laughter! Darrell caught us all off guard with such an unexpected, yet poignantly funny moment. After making it safely back to the room, Darrell was ready to lie down.

I have taken many walks with Darrell through the years, but this particular walk has to be one of the best. Darrell was glad that he could leave his room for the first time since admission, without being pushed in a wheelchair. He may have walked slowly, but we both knew he was beginning to recover.

---

[1]*Compression or anti-embolism stockings*: used to prevent the formation of blood clots

CHAPTER NINETEEN

Memorial Service from Afar

FOR ME TO watch my mother's memorial and viewing service, I had to set my alarm for 4:30 a.m. However, late the evening before, the hospital had a power outage. Sitting in our pitch-dark room, I was deeply concerned that I would miss watching the service if the power was not restored in time. In hopes of finding another Internet connection, I took my laptop to the top floor of the hospital. Sadly, there was no other connection. I returned to the room and asked God for mercy—and electricity. Thankfully, power was restored in time for the service.

When my family called, my brother, John, held the laptop as he walked around, giving us a brief tour of the little chapel. Then he became silent and began to walk slowly down the center aisle toward Mom's casket. Sadness enveloped me as I gazed upon a frail semblance of my mother. When I recognized the cross necklace she often wore, I began to weep. After I regained my composure, I asked John to kiss Mom on the forehead for me, which he sweetly did. John then took the laptop to a side room where my family had gathered, it was separated from the rest of the chapel by a curtain. Although our moods were naturally a bit somber, it was wonderful to say hello—from a distance—to my family.

At the beginning of the service, John muted his laptop speakers to ensure that no unexpected noises or distractions would be heard. They thoughtfully placed the laptop on a chair where I would have been seated in birth order. The memorial service was brief, but pleasant. During the service, someone read a poem that moved me deeply. I immediately searched online and found the words, which I later shared with the rest of the family and my friends. The poem is called, "If Tomorrow Never Comes".

After saying goodbye to my family, I had to purposefully put the service out of my mind so I could sleep. I was emotionally drained and had little time for sleep before the day started.

After breakfast and a busy morning of therapy and nurse visits, I told Darrell that I needed to rest. Right as I had settled in, a hospital staff-woman entered our room with a very stern look on her face. She walked over to me and, without saying a word, handed me a stack of papers. She immediately turned around and left the room. Confused, I looked down at the papers and saw they were hospital bills. I was startled to see how much I owed! The "total due" was for the surgery, two days in the ICU and every medicine and supply used. Since it was posted in their currency, and with the exchange rate, it made for a shockingly large number.

Tired and emotional, I began to cry. Coming immediately on the heels of my mom's memorial service, knowing I was about to miss her funeral, receiving the hospital bill was too much for my sleep-deprived mind. As tears streamed down my face, I stared at the papers in disbelief. While Darrell quietly rested, I felt the tremendous weight on my shoulders: taking care of Darrell, keeping an eye on the doctor, and now bearing the financial responsibility of the whole ordeal. I had not truly considered the financial aspect until I received that second bill.

Wayne was extremely supportive, escorting me to the cashier's office and helping me with the exchange rate. The hospital did accept credit cards, and thankfully, we carried more than one. With two surgeries, daily room charges, ICU charges, meals, medicines, and the like, my credit card quickly reached its limit. Every two days, someone from the business office brought me a new bill, and every two days I would pay that bill. Each visit to the cashier's cage, I reread the same sign proclaiming cash payment for the surgeon's fees was required. I voiced my concerns to Wayne regarding the little cash I had available. I began to wonder if the surgeon's fees pertained only to the surgeries themselves, or if each visit the doctor made to our room and the ICU also applied.

Tom learned of the financial situation we faced. Unbeknownst to us, he sent an email asking friends to consider helping us. We learned that Wayne and Louise had a mission board in the States that was able to wire money for urgent matters such as ours. A couple of dear friends and three churches came to our financial aid. With sympathetic hearts, they sent love-offerings to help our seemingly hopeless situation. Wayne converted their gifts to local currency and set it aside for the cash-only surgeon fees.

Every few days I asked the doctor if he had an estimate of his fees. He never acknowledged my inquiry, which left me feeling unprepared and extremely unsettled. The doctor's total bill would remain a mystery until Darrell's final discharge. This uncertainty was a great burden, and I desperately longed for the financial wisdom and comfort of my mother's voice.

CHAPTER TWENTY

Our Doctor Stoops to a New Low

UNFORTUNATELY, DARRELL'S POST-SURGICAL care was provided by the same doctor who had delayed my husband's original, desperate need for treatment. Every time that doctor walked into our room, I made sure to watch his every movement—very closely. As the doctor removed the bandages covering Darrell's wounds, I cringed. This doctor never washed his hands, and he never used gloves. Much to my dismay while inspecting the surgical site, he touched Darrell's wounds. I had no idea what the doctor's hands had touched prior to walking into our room. I found his lack of hygiene very disturbing.

I knew this touching of the wound could be detrimental to Darrell's health, and as much as I wanted to stop the doctor, I was simply too afraid of him. If Darrell required further surgery and this doctor would perform it, I did not want my actions to make the already frightening situation any worse.

The first time the doctor uncovered Darrell's wound, I was stunned by what I saw. Forty-five staples held a long S-shaped incision closed. Multiple small clusters of stitches closed the incisions from the laparoscopic surgery. Lastly, I saw the colostomy bag as well as the multiple drainage tubes. To see the stark signs of what his body had been through was both sad and shocking.

After the wound check, the doctor pulled back the covers even further to look at Darrell's groin area. I watched him closely, not understanding why he felt the need to check further. I wondered if the doctor was curious because Darrell was so tall compared to the people of Eden. Every day I watched the doctor check Darrell's wounds and touch them with his unwashed, ungloved hands. Then the doctor would discreetly check my husband's groin area. I finally decided there must be some reason for his concern. After all, he was a medical doctor, and he should know what to check. At this point in his recovery, Darrell still had a catheter and was completely bed bound, except for the brief moments of standing or walking under the direction of the physical therapist.

On the second day of this strange inspection, a situation arose of unbelievable, bad timing. The hospital always delivered an English edition of the daily newspaper to our room. Up to this point, we had chosen to stop reading the newspaper. Often the front page had articles about the severe dengue fever outbreak and stories of foreigners being abducted. We did not need to concentrate on negative news with everything else we were facing.

This particular day, I failed to even notice the newspaper's headline, which screamed in big, bold letters, "U.S. JETS INVADE EDEN'S AIRSPACE!" The doctor, however, made sure we knew that he had seen it. After entering our room with his arms tightly crossed, he dramatically leaned over the end of the bed looking towards the newspaper on the table, and then stared at the headline for an incredibly long time. There was an awkward silence when I finally saw what he was staring at, followed by a deep feeling of dread.

The doctor finally lifted his eyes from the paper and made a loud, long, frustrated sigh. He looked at Darrell with a look of disgust. His slow turn and loud sigh seemed to shout silently "U.S. jet—U.S. officer, U.S jet—U.S. officer, you are one and the same. You are the enemy!"

With his slow swagger and air of disrespect for my husband, the doctor continued his follow-up treatment of Darrell. He continued to check my husband's wound and groin area for a few more days, while periodically putting down the American healthcare system. We simply bit our tongues and said nothing.

One day I noticed that Darrell's face looked as if he was in pain. When I inquired, he told me that he felt very uncomfortable. Surprised, I asked him what he meant, knowing he was still on heavy pain medication. Darrell pointed to the area that the doctor had been checking every day. As I pulled back the covers, to my horror, I saw that his scrotum was swollen to the size of a cantaloupe! To say I was shocked would have been an understatement. I had no idea that was even possible!! I was honestly afraid—beyond frightened—that it was going to burst. I tended to Darrell closely to make him comfortable—to no avail. He was miserable.

When the doctor returned to our room the following day, I exclaimed, "Doctor, something is very wrong, Darrell is extremely swollen!" As I pulled back the covers to show the doctor, he said in a calm, uncaring tone, "Oh, that's just a protein deficiency."

I realize *now* that the doctor had been aware of the condition. He had been silently watching its progress because I had seen him checking it every single day. A protein deficiency?! He had *never once* urged Darrell to eat protein; in fact, Darrell's diet consisted of jello, pudding, cake, mashed potatoes, and the like at every meal. Basically, his meals had little to no protein at all.

I can only explain that what happened next is God placed a veil of sorts over my understanding. God knows that I, in my normal state, would have become very pro-active in how I handled this abuse. I am "my father's daughter" and by nature, I'm a defender of the helpless. I will always speak up for those being mistreated, bullied—especially a family member! Had I been in my normal, unveiled state, I would have taken *great* pleasure in blocking the door the next time he came to "treat" my husband! I would have requested a new doctor, and I would have contacted our U.S. embassy.

Here was a doctor who, by all appearances, was purposely contributing to the suffering of his patient—simply because the patient was a Christian/retired American serviceman. He was not *treating* him as a patient; rather, he was enjoying watching him *suffer* as a so-called enemy.

So, why would God put a veil over my understanding? Maybe because of this: Our new missionary friends were in our hospital room every day. This particular doctor and the hospital staff had seen them many times. If the U.S. embassy had been called, Wayne and Louise would likely have been requested to appear as witnesses. With the negative attention this would have caused, and knowing they were friends with us being U.S. missionaries, it's very likely that they would have been asked to leave the country. This missionary family has served faithfully in Eden for many years, so it would have been tragic for my natural defending reactions to cause such a wonderful ministry to end. I believe with *all of my heart* that God allowed this lack of understanding to come over me until we were completely out of the country.

Shortly after our return to U.S. soil (when it was too late to do anything about my husband's abuse), my understanding suddenly cleared. With amazing, clear acuity, I realized that the doctor had vengefully allowed this to happen. It is still almost inconceivable for me to think that the horrific suffering my Darrell endured was wholly intentional.

As a medical professional, I am appalled that such reprehensible abuse and neglect should be inflicted upon any human being...especially in the name of medicine! As someone who actually knows this kind and gentle man, I felt physically sickened by the mere reading of these events. This was truly a hate crime against one of our very own American heroes.

– Name Withheld, RN, BSN

CHAPTER TWENTY-ONE

Recovery Therapy

DARRELL REMAINED UNUSUALLY quiet after his surgery. The trauma of the surgery itself coupled with the raging infection had left him extremely weak. I was concerned that the additional emotional stress of my mom's passing would be too much, so I determined to avoid mentioning my own deep grief. I knew his recovery would take a long while, and my desire was to help, not hinder, his recuperation.

On occasion, Darrell asked me to read from the Bible. He especially liked me to read from the book of Psalms. I relished the opportunity to read to him the promises from this amazing book; they were comforting for both of us. As I would settle in to read some beautiful verses, Darrell would interrupt me after reading only a few, saying, "Thank you, honey. That's enough." In his weakened condition, it was exhausting for him to simply lie in bed and listen for more than a few minutes. It broke my heart to see him so weak.

To my surprise, he asked me for another favor—for us to sing. The funny thing is…I am tone deaf. I know a few songs very well that I can sing halfway decently, but most of the time, my notes only hit "near" their intended mark. There we were—no piano accompaniment, no song book, one tone-deaf singer, and one so weak you could hardly even hear him. But we sang.

He asked me to sing, and boy, did I sing—like a canary! Well, maybe not exactly like a canary. Adding to this unprofessional moment, our 50-plus year-old memories shuffled a few of the verses around. We happily hummed the words we forgot and continued singing in our exhausted condition. Talent may not have reigned that night in room 901, but we rejoiced while singing the great hymns of the faith. What inspirational therapy that was to our weary, battered souls.

We were both excited the day Darrell was finally cleared to drink their amazing tea! To make this much-longed-for moment even more spectacular, Darrell walked gingerly to the table. He wanted to enjoy his first cup sitting down. He was so happy that he even asked me to take his picture!

The missionary brought us gospel tracts in the three languages spoken in Eden. We placed them in neat stacks on one of the bedside tables, almost on display. As hospital workers learned of an American who didn't quite fit in the bed, and how his blonde wife's mother passed away halfway around the world as we were in their hospital, they peered into our room to observe us. I would always wave, give them a big smile, and say "hello." I often waved for them to come in. Suddenly, they started to come into our room in groups asking for tracts! Most of them did not speak English, so they would excitedly point to the tract in the language they could read. With wonder at this incredible new happening, I smiled, emphatically shaking my head, "Yes."

A few of the nurses spoke English, and they came in our room to talk to me. As I explained why we had come to Eden, they were deeply moved. I was humbled and delighted to lead six of the nurses to the Lord at the foot of Darrell's bed.

One day, a male hospital worker came repeatedly to our room. He brought me different items: juice, water, more juice, folded napkins, and more items for which I had not even asked. As he placed the items on the table, he made a gentle bow and smiled broadly as he backed away. As I questioned in my mind why I was suddenly receiving such royal treatment, I finally saw what interested him.

He repeatedly glanced at the tray with the tracts! I motioned with my hand as if to offer one, and his smile somehow beamed more brightly! He grabbed one of the tracts and whisked out the door.

I find it so wonderful that God is not limited to church buildings, He was right there with us in the hospital. We were able to share His love with those whose long work hours may have kept them from ever attending a church service. He allowed us to minister to their spiritual needs—even as He used them to minister to our physical needs. Amazing!

Once we finally knew it was protein that Darrell so desperately needed, George, who worked in the hospital kitchen, made his way to our room daily. George spoke English very well, having worked previously at an international hotel. Since he was accustomed to interacting with foreigners, he would ask Darrell if he had a special request. With Darrell's appetite almost nonexistent, George always wanted to prepare something that would be hard for him to resist. He even offered to cook chicken nuggets, which was not on the hospital menu. He was so kind to us!

One day, George asked us what we were doing in Eden. As soon as I indicated we were missionaries, he told us that his wife and son were both born-again Christians. "Maybe one day," he added, "when I am good enough, I can be saved, too."

I gently told him, "George, you will never be good enough to be saved because we will never be good enough to save ourselves." I offered to show him how he could have assurance that he was going to Heaven some day when this life has ended. However, he declined, explaining that Darrell's food was getting cold. When I told him we cared little for the temperature of our food, he bowed and as he left, he promised to let me show him another time.

Another day as I gazed down over our balcony, I saw the beautiful people of Eden walking on the street below. My heart yearned to meet them and to talk to them about their enchanting country. I also wanted to tell them about Christ, the One who had created it all! I was surprised to see that some people noticed the blonde lady standing on the ninth-story balcony. They waved, and I happily waved back at them.

Suddenly, I had an idea, but I wanted to ask Louise first. "Is it proper to fold a Gospel tract?"

She replied, "Yes."

I grabbed two stacks of the non-English tracts, and after I folded them twice, I dropped them, one at a time, over my balcony toward the pedestrians below. The reaction was unbelievable! People would stop traffic to pick them up, and they would walk away slowly, reading them. A few caught the wind and blew back over the five-foot wall of the hospital, but that did not deter the many men who quickly hopped over the wall to get them! Occasionally when I threw a tract as hard as I could so that it would go farther, the wind blew it right back at me. I could not contain my laughter. What priceless therapy!

I suddenly realized that we had experienced an amazing turn of events. It appeared as if the frightening storm we faced was *finally* beginning to pass. It was as though I could see beautiful rays of light breaking through the dark, stormy clouds that surrounded us, and I was reminded that we were still on a mission trip.

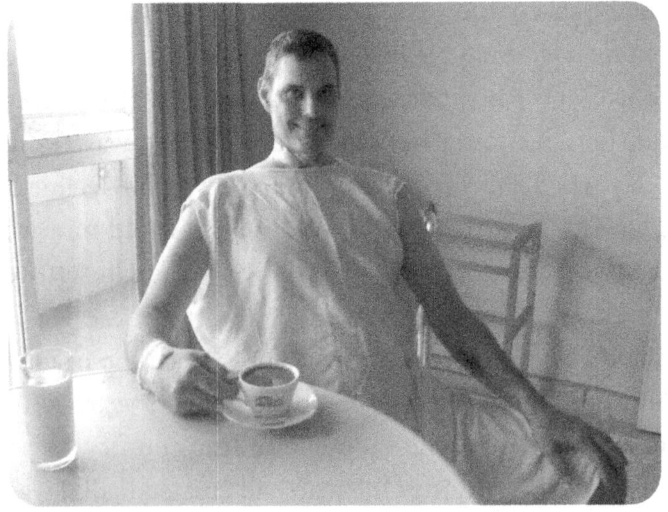

The much-awaited first cup!

CHAPTER TWENTY-TWO

Just an Observation

I NOTICED SOMETHING interesting about the gentle, loving people in Eden. A particular tradition seemed completely contrary to their sweet nature. Because most of them are Buddhist, they will not kill anything for any reason. Yet at times, this practice seemed to be more cruel than kind.

One morning while I was resting in the hospital, I was awakened by a loud, high-pitched yelping. This awful sound was the kind that sends a chill down your spine. Running to the balcony, I saw a dog that had been hit by a car. This poor dog was in extreme pain, and my heart was broken to see and hear the wounded animal. However, many people—men and women alike—walked casually past the pain-ridden animal. Putting him down was not an option, even though he suffered greatly. Because Buddhists believe in reincarnation, in their minds that maimed dog could possibly be a relative. Since they would never dream of killing a relative, they simply let nature take its course. In this particular case, nature was almost unbearable to witness.

Another event that occurred during the month we were in Eden was a severe dengue fever outbreak which swept through the country. Eventually, the authorities did fine and jail those who left standing water on their property, but those in authority would never, ever consider the use of pesticides to save their people from a painful and deadly disease. Wayne told us of the agony the people endured when they contracted the fever. Despite the growing number of Eden's citizens who perished or were hospitalized, they would never consider killing the mosquitoes responsible for the spread of the disease, as they too might be a reincarnated relative. A few years later I would contract dengue fever during an outbreak in the Philippines, and I was thankful that my immune system was strong enough to fight it.

We were told another remarkable story involving the mosquito. It was about a young man we met while in Eden, whom I will call Peter. Wayne had spent several months witnessing to this young Buddhist man. One day, while Wayne and another man visited Peter, a mosquito landed on the man's arm. Instinctively, he swatted it. In outrage, Peter jumped up and yelled for them to leave. He could not believe their cruelty—they had killed a mosquito!

However, Peter knew there was something very different about those men; he could sense something very real in their lives. He later contacted Wayne, telling him that he wanted to get together and speak again. When Wayne arrived, Peter told him that nobody had ever shown him love like Wayne had shown him. That day he understood the gospel and accepted Christ as his Savior. Peter is now the pastor and interpreter for one of the non-English church services! In fact, Peter was one of the men who anointed Darrell with oil, and his precious wife interpreted for me as I taught the ladies' class.

CHAPTER TWENTY-THREE

Discharged— My New Favorite Word!

FINALLY, THE DAY came when the doctor told us that Darrell was improving so well that his discharge was imminent. What tremendous news to hear! He also told us that we needed to stay in Eden a short while longer to schedule an appointment to remove the staples holding his incision closed. He also gave us the business card of a medical supply representative who would teach us how to care for Darrell's colostomy and sell us the supplies we would need.

Since Darrell's body had been ravaged with infection, I asked if he could have oral antibiotics until we made it to the U.S. After writing a prescription for two types of antibiotics, the doctor, in a very serious manner, asked some very strange questions.

"What kind of training did the military give you?" he asked. "Because your body…(as he looked up and down Darrell's body as he sat in a wheel chair)…it's as if you are Superman."

Darrell replied, "No, there was no special training."

The doctor continued in a serious manner. "Really, there was no special training? Your body, I don't understand it; it's like you are Superman."

Darrell repeated his first answer, "No, nothing special."

That was not the end of the questioning. The doctor later returned to the room a second time with more questions. This time he asked, "So…do you have a special exercise regimen? Darrell replied that he had done some regular jogging throughout the years, but that he was not very serious about exercising. Again, the doctor referred to Darrell as Superman.

The doctor returned a third time, asking, "Do you take a lot of vitamins?"

This time I laughed, saying, "No, that would be me who takes all the vitamins!" Once again, the doctor compared Darrell to Superman and then returned to his duties.

At the time we did not understand the doctor's line of thinking when he grilled us about Darrell's physical stamina. Later, however, when we realized the truth about the treatment Darrell needed but did not receive, everything started to fall into place in our minds. As we shared this story with friends and medical personnel here in the States, we all came to the same conclusion: the doctor was baffled that Darrell did not die! By all accounts, he should have. As someone put it, "He asked because he could not successfully kill him!"

The only explanation I have is that God, the Great Physician, has more work for Darrell to accomplish. And our loving Heavenly Father had pity for me in my great loss. He would not allow more grief in my life than I could bear. Neither a doctor in Eden, nor anyone else, is able to alter God's plan. He is *always able* to reach down to help His children and is quite capable of working a miracle if needed. We are so thankful for His amazing power and mercy!

Late that afternoon, we received a glorious update! The sister-nurse (similar to an RN) informed us that Darrell would be released from the hospital that very night! We called Wayne and Louise with the good news.

Our once-quiet night was suddenly busy with the excitement of packing! We also experienced conflicted feelings. Indeed, the previous 16 days had brought heartbreak, fear, and frustration; yet these days had also brought us laughter, gracious kindness from several people, and many answers to prayer.

One may think that we would have wanted to run from that hospital as fast as we could and never look back. However, when we remembered everything that had happened, leaving was truly bittersweet.

Shortly before we left the hospital, I called George the chef, telling him we had an earlier discharge than planned. He begged, "Please don't leave until I can come up to see you!" Within an hour, George was sitting on our sofa. He listened intently as I explained how he could be assured of a home in Heaven; then George sweetly asked the Lord to save him. Immediately afterward, he grinned as he devised a plan. He asked me to call his wife to share the wonderful news. He gave me his home telephone number, asking me to call after 10:30 that night. What an exciting call that was to make, and I honestly could not stop my eyes from crying happy tears. As you can imagine, his wife was absolutely thrilled with the news!

With an ever-growing feeling of suspense, Wayne and I finally headed to the cashier's area to learn the grand total of the surgeon's fees. Despite the generous love offerings that had been sent to us, we still did not have enough cash to cover the balance due. I explained to the cashier that we had come to Eden to help the people; and without a local bank, I could not acquire any more cash. Thankfully, they accepted our credit card, and we were free (no pun intended) to leave the hospital.

After gathering our things, the nurse rolled Darrell out of the room in a wheelchair. We made a stop at the nurses' station where we were greeted by the teary-eyed staff. We were touched to see their sad emotions as their foreigner patient and his wife were finally leaving their hospital. On his day of departure, Darrell stood up to say goodbye to the wonderful people who so graciously cared for him, and he was shocked to see how short the people actually were! Because he had spent the majority of his time lying horizontal in bed, he had not noticed their short stature. His animated reaction to how small they were made for a fun final memory. Thankfully, his jovial comments replaced their sad faces with smiles. After taking pictures, exchanging email addresses and receiving hugs, we could clearly see that the nurses were sad to see us leave.

As I watched Darrell slowly make his way to the car, I felt a tremendous weight drop off my shoulders. My husband had survived, and he was truly leaving the hospital.

CHAPTER TWENTY-FOUR

The Last Days in Eden

A HUGE SENSE of relief swept over us as we walked into Wayne's home, knowing that the grueling hospital stay and two surgeries were finally behind us. My first task was to purchase our airline tickets to Thailand. The second doctor had made it clear that Darrell was not ready for the extended flight back to the States. He had recommended that we stay in Thailand a minimum of five days, to make sure Darrell was strong enough for the longest leg of our journey home.

I was thrilled to be going to a new country and even more thrilled to see several friends who lived there. We hadn't seen them in years! Our friends had been extremely encouraging throughout our recent trial, and we longed to be with them. I was also eager to meet the Thai family who would be hosting us. From taking previous missions trips to Thailand, Darrell already knew this dear family and loved them very much.

After purchasing our tickets from Thai Airlines, we said goodnight to Wayne and Louise. For the first time in weeks, I was thrilled to actually sleep next to Darrell—and in the same bed.

Darrell felt fairly good after his first uninterrupted night's sleep, so that morning he encouraged me to join Wayne and Louise who were heading out to invite people to church and hand out tracts. I could not help but smile as I greeted the wonderful people of Eden. Once again, the weather was extremely hot, so I sought out shade whenever possible. As I looked around, I saw a partially opened curtain in the doorway of a very small room. Inside, I could see an elderly lady waving at us. We approached the room and as I pulled back the curtain, I was shocked at what my eyes beheld.

This sweet lady had been left alone in a stuffy, hot room with no air flow. The room was not much larger than the unkempt little bed in which she lay. Her feet were plainly visible, and I saw that most of her toes had been eaten away with disease, and they were mangled by some deformity. She tenderly reached for this blonde stranger, and though I longed to embrace her, her disintegrating toes seemed to shout, "Leprosy!" If that were the case, I knew I dared not touch her.

In broken English, she said, "I can't get up." In effect, she was held captive with a makeshift catheter in a foul-smelling room. Continuing to reach for me, she lifted her head which revealed dried blood on her dirty pillowcase. My heart literally ached within me.

My translator and I tried to share the Gospel with her, but she continued to ask questions about me. She wanted to know from where I came. If we mentioned Heaven, she wanted to know when I was going and if I could take her with me. She seemed to be losing some of her ability to reason. She told my translator that she would ask her daughter to read the Gospel tract in her native tongue.

She continued to reach for me, and I desperately longed to sit and stroke her hair. My heart wanted to do something to make the remaining days of her life more comfortable. Though it was beyond my ability to do that for her earthly body, I knew the tract we gave her held the information she needed to ensure her comfort and peace in the next life.

I walked away from that pitiful sight with a painful lump in my throat, silently praying that God would use the tract to turn the lady (and her daughter) to Him. Then she wouldn't have to rely on a blonde stranger to take her to Heaven, but rather God Who loved her so very much.

We continued to walk, passing through a predominantly Muslim area. The people in the Muslim community were not as open to the

Gospel. In fact, one group of men seemed angry and began to shout something at us. I wasn't sure what they were saying, but my translator knew. She explained that they planned to stone us if we did not leave. We decided to continue walking—quickly!

When we returned to the house, I shared our experiences with Darrell over lunch. That afternoon we relaxed and took in the beauty of the wildlife and gorgeous foliage around the backyard patio. That day the birds' songs seemed a little sweeter and the sunset even more spectacular.

Darrell awoke Sunday morning feeling strong enough to go to church. When we arrived, he was overwhelmed by the displays of genuine love that were lavished on him. He was welcomed by everyone. One man had made Darrell an avocado shake, explaining that it was packed with nutrients essential for his recovery. He loved it. I was glad Darrell was able to meet the ladies and teen girls whom I had enjoyed getting to know.

That morning we also met the owner of the amazing house in which Wayne and Louise live. This kind, generous man lives abroad, but he happened to be in town the same Sunday we were there. Darrell shook his hand and without letting go, proceeded to weep all over it.

Darrell thanked him (between sobs) for sharing his home…which, in turn, was then shared with us. It was more than a home to us; it had become a special place of healing and emotional restoration. No words could adequately describe what that haven meant to us. After Darrell's deep expression of thanks, the man related an experience of his own. We learned that following a bomb blast at his office years earlier, he too had personally experienced the amazing power and grace of God. He now lives his life putting people before *things*—which is a *beautiful* way to live. What an honor to meet him and personally thank him for his generosity! After a wonderful service and a heartfelt, "Thank you," we bid the precious people a tearful goodbye.

On Monday, two days before we were to leave, Wayne and Louise took us to a multi-level souvenir store. We enjoyed seeing the local handmade items, but Darrell tired quite easily, requiring multiple breaks. After purchasing a few unique items, we were given a fascinating personal tour of the area. While seated in the comfort of their van, we drank in the sights and listened to interesting stories about the history of the region. We saw mosques with their magnificent domed architecture. Then we gazed in amazement at the intricacies of the architecture of the Buddhist temples. Our moods grew more solemn as they pointed out areas of military attacks and battles from years past. We even stopped at a park to see the enormous fruit bats as they slept in the trees!

Our incredible tour ended with a mid-afternoon buffet at a lovely resort hotel. The food was amazing, and the outdoor restaurant had a gorgeous backdrop—the Indian Ocean! As we finished our fabulous meal, the waiter reappeared. On his tray he carried a beautiful formal tea service, from which he served each of us a cup of their spectacular tea! I knew better than to have caffeine past noon, but I could not resist. Knowing I was about to leave the country, I abandoned my better judgment and savored every sip (Twice! I had two cups!). Louise and I then took a short walk on the wooden deck behind the restaurant to get a closer look at the ocean. We were enjoying the stunning view when suddenly a wave came crashing over the wall, spraying us both! Giggling as we ran away, I was surprised to hear myself laugh aloud. What a difference a few days, and a spray of ocean water can make.

After a memorable day, we returned to our "oasis"—as we lovingly called their home. As our departure was now less than 48 hours away, we began to pack. With my back condition and Darrell's need for wheelchair assistance, I now looked at our things in a much different light. Luggage I once loved was now too heavy, and once-cherished items were now a burden. For the sake of traveling light, I left many belongings behind.

After packing, we settled into bed, but I was immediately reminded of my caffeine intolerance—and the two cups of tea I had enjoyed that afternoon. I tossed and turned all night, and at five in the morning I regretted not only my second cup of tea, but even my first! Our flight to Thailand the following night was at 1:00 am. Knowing I faced another night of virtually no sleep, I asked myself, "What were you thinking!?"

Darrell woke up long before anyone else and sat outside with his coffee. As dawn began to break, a beautiful bird flew toward him, landing on the concrete wall surrounding the property. Darrell smiled, leaned toward the bird and said, "Hi, beautiful bird! I know Who made you! Jesus made you!" Soon, another beautifully colored bird flew into the yard. Grinning, Darrell turned toward that bird and greeted it with a cheerful hello.

Later, I carried my coffee outside and joined him in his birdwatching. The birds were not only beautiful; they were species we had never seen or even heard of before. They were colorful, unique, and truly spectacular. Darrell often cried—everything was so beautiful!

He wept with a thankful heart over all the miracles that God had accomplished for us during those 16 trying days. He wept, reflecting on how wonderfully Wayne and Louise cared for us. He wept at the splendor of the beauty that was all around us—the birds, the rice fields, the flowers, everything! I teased that maybe there was a little morphine still in his system. For one reason or another, his heart was amazingly tender, and I loved it.

As we sat outside together, monkeys became our therapy. One morning they playfully climbed across the roof and over the wall. They jumped and swung from tree to tree, showing off their innate acrobatic skills. Wanting to capture the monkeys on video, I had to lure them out of the trees. I resorted to bribery, by sticking a banana between the rungs of the metal gate. I ran to the front door and, with camera rolling, I captured the scene when a monkey spied the banana. He came down from the trees and stopped at the top of the wall. He looked down, almost reeling at the temptation of his favorite food. He quickly glanced at the door where I was standing. Finally deciding that the banana was worth the risk, he scurried down to the gate. He grabbed the banana, popped it into his mouth, and then scampered to the safety of the branches. I laughed as he disappeared into the trees with his treasure.*

After our fill of monkeys and a fantastic lunch Louise had prepared, we realized that we needed to finish packing. Darrell and I talked about our new-found friends, Wayne, Louise, and Jeremy. They were a remarkable family with caring, selfless hearts. Wishing we could do more, we prepared two thank you notes. The first had a little offering for them to use for their upcoming Vacation Bible School program. The other note was strictly for comic relief. It also contained a little money with a funny list of things to use it for—in reality, to help with all the extra food, electricity, McTherapy, phone calls, gasoline, parking fees…and more McTherapy!

On our last afternoon in Eden, Darrell had one final doctor's appointment to have his staples removed. What a great feeling we had as we walked away from that hospital, knowing we did not have to go back. We gathered our bags and, with a plethora of emotions, loaded the van. We felt joy in heading home as well as excitement to see our friends in Thailand. Then there was sadness to leave our special new friends, but gladness to see our family. And definitely, we felt a dread in facing the reality that I'd truly lost my mom.

On the way to the airport, we stopped at a restaurant. While we were eating, Louise gave us a card and asked us not to open it until we boarded the plane. Arriving at the airport, we shared our emotional goodbyes. This family will never know how much they mean to us. After we thanked them for the love they had shown, we walked away, wiping our tears. We came as strangers—we left as friends.

When the time came to check our baggage, the airline agent informed us that two of our suitcases were overweight, requiring fees. I explained to her that our suitcases held stacks of medical bills, a folder filled with all the pictures from Darrell's CAT scans and his ultrasound, as well as medical supplies. Just one glimpse of my weak husband in a wheelchair, and she chose to let our bags go without charge. I was overwhelmed at the many ways compassion was shown to us.

I wheeled Darrell slowly around the little airport gift shops to pass the time until our 1:00 a.m. flight. As the plane ascended, we opened the card Louise had given us. Unbeknownst to us, they had peeked in the cards we gave them at the house. While they accepted the money for their VBS, they refused the money in the second card. She wrote a note that brought us both to tears. It read, "One day we will be able to sing and enjoy Heaven for all of eternity. But it is only here on earth that we can love, serve, and minister one to another as unto the Lord."

Our new friends—easily mistaken for angels.

---

*A delightful video of the monkey's antics is posted on the book's website, www.withunwashedhands.com.

CHAPTER TWENTY-FIVE

Arriving in Thailand

After my over-indulgence of tea which had left me sleepless the previous night, I was looking forward to settling down to sleep on the overnight flight. We learned that there was a downside to the exceptional service on foreign flights. The airline served hot curry meals! (Of course, what else would it be?) I do not know how many people can sleep through the aroma of a curry-filled plane, but I quickly discovered that I am not one of them. The thought of eating curried fish at 3:00 a.m. was far from appetizing.

After landing safely in Thailand, we experienced the only perk of traveling with a husband in a wheelchair—priority service through customs and immigration. The medical help we requested ushered us past the long lines. The gentleman pushing Darrell even completed our customs forms for us. After making our way past customs and baggage claim, we went to the meeting area to wait for our Thai host, Pastor Jomhong. The back-to-back nights of very little sleep caused me to look longingly at the airport floor. I saved Darrell the embarrassment and remained upright.

I was excited to meet Pastor Jomhong; the three of us chatted as he drove us to the Diamond Place Hotel. As we checked in, we discovered that the name of the hotel sounds much fancier than it really is. We were glad to see Tom again; he had just arrived in Thailand several hours before us. Mrs. Jomhong, or Khun Siriporn, as they call her in Thailand, brought pancakes for breakfast. Since we did not eat the curry fish in the middle of the night, we were famished by 10:00 a.m.!

After the delicious breakfast, we told Tom we needed to take a brief nap. However, due to our excitement, we didn't nap long. Believe it or not, merely being away from the hospital was still new and exciting to us, and we also were about to renew old friendships! Additionally, we found it hard to sleep with the sun shining bright.

We talked with Tom until the Jomhongs picked us up for an early dinner at their lovely home. They told us how much they prayed for us when they heard what had happened. We decided not to share with anyone the medical horrors that Darrell had faced. We simply were not ready.

Darrell and I were excited to go to church that night. From the car, I noticed signs written in Thai, with their beautiful scrolling letters. As we walked into the church, I immediately noticed a sweet-faced teenage girl standing near the entrance. She stood with tears in her eyes and hands by her mouth. She seemed excited to see Darrell and then became visibly emotional to see him so frail.

As Darrell walked gingerly toward a chair to sit down, she approached him to tell him she had cried and prayed for him every day. Those words were wonderful to hear, yet extremely humbling. (Darrell and I were amazed at how many people told us that they had prayed for us. Person after person informed us that they had put us on their church's prayer lists in cities all over our nation. In fact, we heard from cities from around the world! We were amazed to hear from so many people who told us that they had shared our circumstances with others, and in a matter of hours, scores of strangers were praying on our behalf.)

When the service started, everyone began to sing in Thai. We simply smiled and sang the familiar songs in English. After a song or two, the sweet girl I had noticed earlier ascended the platform to sing a special. After hearing only a few notes, I recognized the song that was playing. I let out an audible gasp and began to cry. It was a tender song titled "He Is There," which was written by Amber Guzzi, a beautiful young lady whom we know personally. She penned this heartfelt song while her newlywed husband, Matt, was going through treatment for terminal cancer. Soon Darrell was crying, and then even the sweet little soloist cried as she continued to sing this very special song. (The lyrics are in the appendix.)

Pastor Jomhong asked Darrell to give a testimony, and after sharing a brief update, he preached his entire sermon. Darrell's spirit was great, and he was so very happy! He preached a fun message that had some of us getting involved. The Pastor's brother also preached a full sermon, making it a very late night.

When we finally returned to our hotel, Tom wanted to get something to eat. Before I could say, "I am much too tired to eat," Darrell blurted, "Yeah, let's do that!" With a two-to-one vote, we ate at the little restaurant in the Diamond Place. After eating, we went to our rooms, exhausted.

As we settled in for the night, I remembered that Tom had a phone, so I ran next door to ask if I could borrow it. With Darrell tucked safely into bed, I was about to make a phone call—a phone call that would, quite literally, change our lives.

CHAPTER TWENTY-SIX

Another Hospital?!

When I suddenly remembered that Tom had a phone, Darrell was already settled in one of our room's "Lucy & Ricky Ricardo" furnishings—twin beds. After my Monday night caffeine issues, flying all night Tuesday, and a busy Wednesday, I honestly should have collapsed into my bed as well. Even though it was after 11:30 p.m., I felt a strong urgency to call Mary Jo, our PA back home in Florida, to explain what had happened to Darrell. I also wanted to have her start the referral process to see a surgeon for a colostomy reversal before we returned the following week. When I told the receptionist I was calling from Thailand, Mary Jo was soon on the phone. I was surprised to find out that a friend of ours had already informed her of our situation.

We spoke for several minutes, and I felt assured that Darrell would be receiving great care once we returned home. As we were about to end our conversation, I said softly to my almost asleep husband, "Honey, can I please see your incision while I have her on the phone?" I know this request had to have been a prompt from the Lord because Mary Jo had not asked me to do it, and I had previously decided to never disturb Darrell if he was resting! Groggily, Darrell pulled down the covers and lifted his shirt. I was aghast as my eyes fixed on a frightening, reddish-brown area on his incision! Terrified of what it could be, I exclaimed, "What is that?! What is that?!"

Hearing the fear in my voice, Mary Jo responded, *"What is what?!"*

Gingerly, I touched the three-inch darkened area and found it hot to the touch. Darrell had *no idea* that he was halfway to sleep with a fevered internal infection! I described to Mary Jo what I saw and felt, and she calmly told me to hang up, call our hosts, and have them take us to the nearest international hospital in Bangkok. She also gave me her personal cell phone number and told me to call her back with an update—no matter the hour.

I ran to tell Tom what was happening, while I frantically called Pastor and Mrs. Jomhong. I was very concerned when each of their cell phones only rang and rang…there was no answer! We did not have a car, and even if we did, we would not know how to get to Bangkok, let alone an international hospital!

I remembered a friend we had met when we were stationed in Omaha, 25 years earlier. Missy, and her husband, Tim, were now missionaries in Thailand! I also happened to have her phone number. When she answered the phone, Missy told me that they had once lived in the Diamond Place Hotel!

Tim, knowing exactly where we were, ran out the door while she and I were still on the phone. I quickly gathered things we would need, but my stomach started to feel very upset. I knew it must be nerves because we were headed back to a hospital. I hated that my being sick hindered our packing.

Tim made great time as he rushed us to a Bangkok hospital and drove us straight to the emergency room door. Taking one look at Darrell's surgical site, the doctor immediately started an IV to administer heavy-dosed antibiotics. After questioning us about the recent surgeries and filling out paperwork, my husband was admitted. We were told that a surgeon would look at him in the morning.

My head was spinning; I could not believe that my poor husband was experiencing this—*again!*

At 3:00 a.m. Tom and I arrived back at the hotel. As we wearily made our way through the lobby, I suddenly remembered that it was 3:00 p.m. back home. It was Wednesday afternoon in America, and people were about to go to church for the midweek service. I imagined the joy of our loved ones giving a praise report, "Darrell and Joanie are *finally* coming home!!" I needed people to know that we were *not* coming home, but that Darrell had an infection and was back in the hospital. We needed people to pray!

I went to a computer in the hotel lobby and in "zombie mode" posted a prayer request update. I spent 30 minutes trying to type one paragraph. In between sentences, and sometimes even words, I had to make repeated trips to the bathroom—as my tummy had serious issues. Dragging myself into my hotel room at 3:30 a.m., I finally climbed into bed—aware that my stomach problems earlier had not been nerves, I was really quite ill. However, for the entire three-and-a-half hours of our hospital trip, including time spent lost driving home from the Bangkok area, I had no problem with my intestinal issue. I thanked God specifically for that kind blessing. I then asked Him to watch over my husband, who was alone in a hospital once again.

I awoke at 6:00 a.m. less than three hours later *extremely* sick with fever, and I was in excruciating pain. Normally, a fever makes me feel cold, however, this time my fever was so high that the skin on my arm seemed to sizzle from heat. With a deep ache in my bones, I could not get out of bed. I tried calling out for help since Tom's room was adjacent to ours. There was no answer. I tried knocking on the wall, hoping to awaken him. With walls made of concrete, all I did was hurt my knuckles.

So there I lay, moaning in pain and wishing there was someone to help me. Two more hours passed, and I finally managed to inch my way out of bed and pull on some clothes. I shuffled, too weak to lift my feet, toward Tom's room, where I was welcomed by a note stuck to the door. The note read, "Joanie, I am downstairs in the lobby working on the computer."

With a despairing sigh, I slowly shuffled back to my room to get a pen. I wrote on his note that I was very sick and unable to go downstairs. At that point, I noticed two cleaning ladies and motioned for help. I spoke to one of them in English, but she shook her head "No," indicating she could not understand me.

I said, "Man," then, "Hat..." (I pretended to put on a hat because Tom always wears a hat.) Then I added, "Wi-fi," and pretended to type.

Still not understanding what I meant, she shook her head again.

Disappointed, I decided to try one more time and repeated, "Man," then "Hat" (pretending to put on a hat) and "Wi-fi," pretending to type.

This time, she made a typing gesture but then quickly shook her head.

Defeated, I turned around. As I started back to my room, I broke down in tears. When she heard me crying, she immediately ran to the elevator and went downstairs. She found Tom in the lobby and said, "The American lady is crying!" in the Thai language, which Tom speaks. I still find it funny that she ran directly to Tom—the "Man" in the "Hat" who was downstairs on the "Wi-fi."

Shortly after I returned to my room, both ladies burst in to take care of me. They carefully laid me on the bed, and strangely, began to massage my body using a Thai technique. Thai massage is interesting... and somewhat painful! With my body already hurting, theirs was not the soothing care I had longed for. Then one of the ladies rubbed a very strong menthol balm on my tummy, arms, legs, and even my nose! She looked at my face and motioned for me to breathe in the fumes. The next thing I knew, she had put some menthol on her finger and stuck her finger inside my nose! I was so hot with fever, I did not care. Tom walked into the room, and once he learned how sick I was, he called the Jomhongs to take me to the hospital.

After going through triage (the process of determining a patient's need for medical care) I was hooked up to an IV and admitted. I had no idea I was running a 104° fever, especially since my normal temperature is in the 96°-97°range! After blood work and testing, I was diagnosed as having an "infection of unknown origin." I would require a couple of days in the hospital with IV antibiotics and steroids.

What a sight that must have been as I was wheeled into Darrell's hospital room. To be sure, this was not how I had planned to visit him that day!

Before my arrival to Darrell's room, Darrell noticed a beautiful butterfly pin adorning one of the nurse's shirts. He commented on how nice it was, telling the nurse that I would like it. "Please show that lovely pin to my wife when she comes to visit." Darrell had no idea that I was sick and was about to be admitted myself!

When the hospital staff settled me in his room, I was still hot with fever experiencing significant pain. I was leaning away from the window and the light. When the nurse returned to our room, Darrell said, "Joanie, look at this beautiful pin!" Honestly, I did not want to turn because of the pain, but I managed to do so. When I saw the pin, I smiled and told the nurse it was beautiful. She immediately took the pin off her lapel and gave it to me. My heart was overwhelmed with her kind thoughtfulness.

Darrell preaching the first night in Thailand;
Pastor Jomhong interpreting

CHAPTER TWENTY-SEVEN

And It's *Back* to the Operating Room!

WHILE LYING IN my hospital bed, I was glad I had sent out the prayer update the night before. Little did I know how far that request would travel, and the surprising turn of events that would take place because of it.

Our daughter-in-law, Beth, happened to read the prayer request before leaving for church in Indiana. She shared the prayer request at church, where her pastor announced that Darrell was back in the hospital in Bangkok, Thailand. Their church service happened to be live-streamed on the Internet, and it happened that a missionary, Dr. Bob Bowen, who also happened to be Darrell's roommate on a previous mission trip, pulled up the church's live-streamed Wednesday night service on his computer.

Surprised to hear the announcement about my husband's unexpected return to a hospital, Dr. Bowen exclaimed, "I know Darrell Bolton, and—I'm in Bangkok, Thailand!" Within a couple of hours, a cheerful Dr. Bowen walked into our room! There are no words to adequately express our utter surprise and delight!

He asked if we wanted anything from the store. We told him we didn't need anything, but he insisted, noting the health benefits of fruit juice. Darrell, an avid juice lover, quickly agreed!

Dr. Bowen asked if I had any favorite snacks. Smiling at his generosity, I assured him that Thailand would not have them. When he insisted, I playfully answered, "Cheetos® and Oreos®!" I thanked him for his kind offer, though I was certain they were not available.

About 20 minutes later, a grinning Dr. Bowen walked back into our room, carrying a bag. He pulled out some amazing tropical fruit juices and placed them on the counter. He then pulled out a bag of Cheetos® and a package of Oreos®! The "Oreo" and "Cheetos" names were in the beautiful Thai scrolled lettering, but I can recognize those product labels anywhere! I could not help but laugh out loud when he tossed them onto my bed!

Not long after his visit, a young Thai doctor walked into our room. His last name is incredibly long, so everyone refers to him as Dr Max. He was very polite and extremely professional as he looked at my husband's surgery sites. Noting the colostomy bag, he asked about Darrell's recent surgeries.

Dr. Max began to examine the infected wound and carefully opened the incision. Within seconds, he announced that Darrell would need another surgery—that evening. Dr. Max explained that the infection had literally burned a hole the size of a quarter in Darrell's abdominal sheath lining! Despite the overnight high dose antibiotics, with the damage the infection had caused, we knew for certain that this surgery was necessary.

I still shudder to think about Darrell lying in that hotel, nearly asleep—content and totally unaware of the burning infection inside his abdomen. I have since questioned: *What if I had not been there? What if Mary Jo were an uncaring, impersonal PA? What if Darrell had roomed alone or with another man? Would a roommate have disturbed his rest to check his wound, especially knowing he was taking two oral antibiotics?* I think not. I believe with *all my heart* that Darrell would have awakened in Heaven, had I not been there. God had known about Darrell's great need long before it happened. He had graciously taken care of everything, down to the smallest detail—*for His glory.*

Tom came to visit that afternoon, and we chuckled at what looked like our sudden penchant for hospitals. Tom teased that he did not want to travel with Darrell anymore, "Because he was always lying around!" His visit helped to pass the time while we waited for Darrell's surgery which, once again, was scheduled to be in the evening.

Tom took a picture of us as we lay side-by-side with our matching IV poles and posted it on Facebook. Our family and friends were relieved when they finally saw Darrell with a big, broad smile.

Shortly before surgery, we were happily surprised to see Dr. Bowen and his wife walk into our room. Without being asked, they chose to sit with me while Darrell was in surgery. Not only was their company refreshing, it was extremely reassuring to me when they took the time to pray out loud… lifting up Darrell and his surgery to God, the Great Physician.

Mrs. Bowen cooled my fever by bringing me cool wash cloths and Tom kindly loaned me his laptop. Their tremendous care helped to keep our family and friends abreast of Darrell's third surgery.

Dr. Bowen took his wife home when it got late, then he picked up my laptop from the hotel and drove all the way back, a 35-minute trip—each way, simply to give it to me! Later, when the projected time for surgery had passed, Dr. Bowen went to get an update at the nurses' station. That kind gesture saved me an embarrassing walk down the hall, wheeling an IV pole in a hospital gown!

At last, someone announced that Darrell had been safely moved from the OR into recovery. Only then did Tom and Dr. Bowen go home. It was long past midnight, and I was very grateful for their sitting with me the entire time my husband was in surgery.

Recovery took longer than they had projected, so I was relieved when Darrell was finally wheeled into our room. The anesthesia left him seemingly unaware of the busy nurses scurrying around his bed. As our room emptied and only the two of us remained, I calmly and quietly watched him rest. I felt thankful that I was not, instead, learning to live without him.

However, my peacefulness was short-lived as Darrell began to moan with pain. I pushed the call button, and the nurse came quickly to the room. Once again, we were faced with a language barrier.

Earlier that day, Dr. Bowen had given us a cell phone with 900 minutes on it. At 2:00 a.m. I was already using it…to wake up Tom. Because Tom speaks Thai, he was able to explain to the nurse that Darrell was hurting very badly. We were glad that our nurses learned at least one English word; they called it "Paining." They had not yet learned the words "severe" and "not going away."

I was becoming upset as I watched Darrell begin to grip his sheets in intense pain. After repeated calls to the nurses' station, the caregivers determined that his pain-dispensing machine was faulty. In the wee hours of the morning, they finally swapped it out. He was also given oxygen to help him relax, and a shot of some sort of pain medicine. After a short time, most of the pain subsided.

Needless to say, Darrell's first night after surgery was a bit rough. We both noticed that the pain management in Thailand was not nearly as effective as it was in Eden.

The following day, Dr. Max returned to fully explain Darrell's surgery. Under the bright lights in the OR he had could clearly see the infection, which he attributed entirely to the dirty conditions in Eden. We were not yet ready to tell Dr. Max, or anybody for that matter, that our first doctor had repeatedly touched Darrell's wounds with his unwashed, ungloved hands.

Darrell's entire incision had to be reopened to clean the area properly. Dr. Max then repaired the sheath by sewing the burned hole closed. Due to the drastic pulling this surgery caused, retention sutures were necessary. Several five-inch-long sutures were encased in a vinyl-like material, laid horizontally across his long incision, with the likeness of a football seam. The retention sutures pulled the entire abdomen together, inward and tight, which would allow the newly closed hole in the sheath to heal.

Dr. Max explained that he had left the wound open to allow draining of the infection. We have since wondered why Darrell's incision was stapled closed in Eden after such a severe case of peritonitis. Much to our dismay, Dr. Max also informed us that Darrell would have a long recovery, requiring our remaining in Thailand for a month. Darrell would have a week-long stay in the hospital, plus three weeks of recovery before going home.

While Darrell's medical update was discouraging, mine was great! My fever had broken, and the IV medicines were taking care of most of the pain. I was happily given a projected discharge date for the next day, but I would continue to take antibiotics and steroids. I was thrilled to know my IV and clear broth days were almost over!

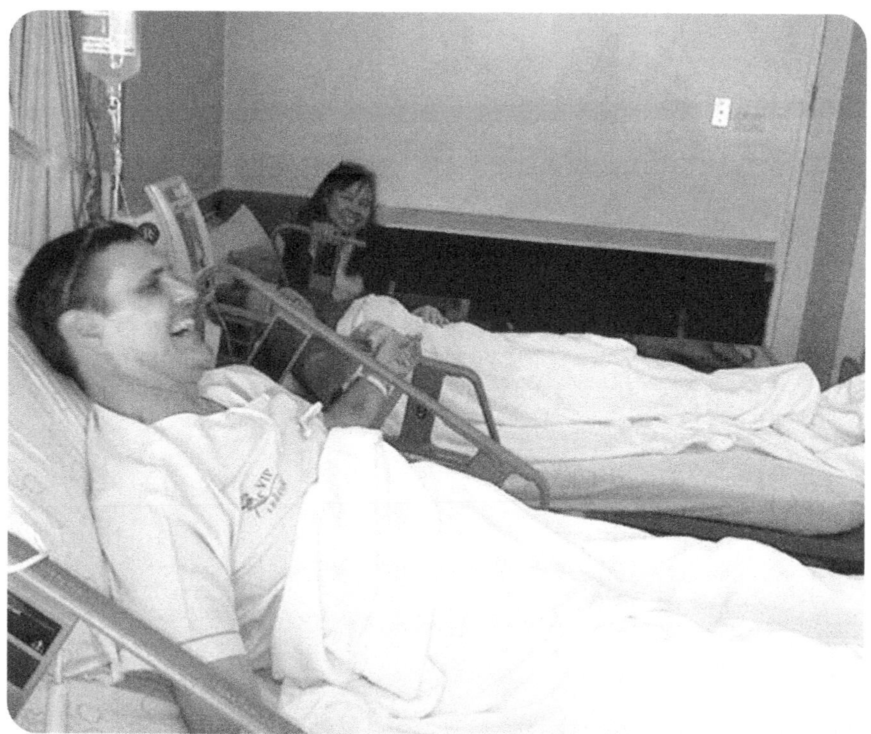

Darrell and Joanie admitted; holding hands (with Mrs. Jomhong in the background)

CHAPTER TWENTY-EIGHT

A Twenty-first Century Good Samaritan

We enjoyed several visitors in the hospital. However, one particular visit was quite out of the ordinary. The Jomhong family wanted to celebrate Mrs. Jomhong's birthday, and since we couldn't leave the hospital, they decided to bring the party to us! Our hearts were delighted by the visit, which consisted of food, flowers, and taking lots of pictures! The best picture was of Mrs. Jomhong and Darrell, who made a sad face while holding a piece of cake he was not allowed to eat.

I was thankful to be untethered from the IV and thankful for the freedom to move about the room. Dr. Bowen and Tom came to take me to the hotel so I could move our belongings to Tom's room, which would save us from paying for an unoccupied room. As I gathered my things in our hotel room, I noticed I was still wearing my hospital bracelet. I had forgotten to tell them when they picked me up that I was not yet discharged. We laughed, imagining frantic hospital workers searching for their missing patient.

As we transferred our items, I saw the two cleaning ladies, who I lovingly call my "menthol nurses." They came over, and with great emotion, we hugged each other. With Tom as my translator, I was able to thank them for being so kind. I had my picture taken with the two ladies, and each time I see it, I fondly recall the unique care I received from those dear ladies…and my failed charades. They told me that my skin had felt so hot, they were afraid I was going to die. Thankfully, I was not nearly as sick as they had thought. As we returned to the hospital, I walked inconspicuously past the nurses' station, and later that afternoon, I was fully released.

With the great care Darrell was receiving, I felt comfortable to go to church on Sunday. Dr. Bowen drove the 35 minutes each way so I could attend services. I was excited to finally see my American friends who live in Thailand. Throughout our ordeal, they had been a great encouragement to us.

After very exciting services, we headed to get some lunch. Along the way, we gave one of the ladies a ride home from church. As we pulled up to her house, I saw one of the most beautiful flowers I had ever seen! They told me it was the lotus flower, and I had a picture taken with it to show how big and gorgeous it was.

The Bowens graciously treated me to lunch. As we sat down in the cafeteria-style restaurant, Dr. Bowen asked me, "Do you want a Coke Zero?"

I had never tasted a Coke Zero before and although it had caffeine, the name sounded so American that I emphatically answered, "Yes!"

He brought me one, and though it was not my favorite drink, it became my favorite for that short period of time. He bought me several during our stay, and it somehow seemed like a little piece of home.

When I returned after lunch, I was relieved to find that the hospital staff was properly taking care of Darrell. He was quite relaxed when I entered the room, but I am not sure how relaxed he stayed after I talked a mile-a-minute about the wonderful day I'd had!

When Darrell was admitted, he was given a self-administered pump used to apply a dose of pain medicine as needed. Unable to read Thai, we simply referred to the medicine as morphine. Despite his use of the pump, Darrell's pain levels did not fully subside. I found it difficult to see him uncomfortable; however, the nurses were gentle and always helped when shots were needed for his "paining." It brought me great peace to see the petite nurses in polished uniforms always wearing gloves.

When we told Dr. Bowen that we'd have to stay in Thailand for three weeks after Darrell's release from the hospital, our "Good Samaritan" sought-out a place for us to stay. He asked a veteran missionary in the area, Shari House, if we could stay in her home. Although she did not know us, she quickly agreed. Darrell and I were very thankful for her hospitality.

Due to the severity of infection in Darrell's body and the increased risk of his having a recurrence, he was required to return to the hospital every day for a dressing change, even after discharge. He was also required to have his wound inspected by a nurse or doctor in the ER. This recommendation was disheartening. Not only did we lack a car, we also did not speak Thai! We could not simply hail a cab or jump on a bus. We felt helpless.

When Dr. Bowen learned of our dilemma, he immediately offered to be our transportation. We were deeply moved that he would care for us in such an amazing way. Over the next few weeks, he told us several times, "I am happy to help."

Besides the many ways he gladly helped us, including a daily hour and ten-minute ride, he made a comment that reminded us of the original Good Samaritan. "You did not ask for this illness, and you did nothing wrong to cause it. I was looking for a wounded man, and there you were."

Above:
The man too tall for his bed!

Below:
My "menthol" nurses

CHAPTER TWENTY-NINE

Darrell Released… Joanie Nearly Evicted!

The pillow on my hospital bed was a bit bizarre; it was hard and made of vinyl. After sleeping on it for a few days, my neck and back were becoming sore. Ironically, the first bit of back pain I had experienced since our long flights in July was caused by a pillow! In addition to the pain, the vinyl material became so hot that I found it difficult to sleep.

I asked one of the nurses if the hospital had any other type of pillow available for the patients. She left to check, and I followed the nurse to a large closet about the size of a small bedroom. She scanned the room and said, "I'm sorry, that is the only pillow…" Before she could finish her sentence, I spied a normal pillow! I lunged into the room and grabbed it, clutching it as a receiver would tightly hold a touchdown pass in the Super Bowl. I thanked her as I turned and quickly walked back to our room.

As the day of Darrell's discharge approached, Dr. Max asked Darrell if he wanted his wound to be left open or stitched closed for a thinner scar line. Darrell chose to have it stitched closed—despite a greater chance of infection. I quietly cringed at his choice but said nothing.

The day came when Darrell was finally taken to the OR where Dr. Max prepared to close the long open incision. Since Darrell was only given local anesthesia, he was awake to hear the noisy procedure. A nurse ran water into the wound and then suctioned it out as Dr. Max carefully stitched it closed. Though a sheet prevented Darrell from seeing the procedure, the sounds he heard were unsettling and made him feel queasy. He began to softly hum some of his favorite hymns to drown out the graphic, gurgling sounds. The procedure lasted much longer than he had imagined it would. He was very glad when Dr. Max and his nurse finished, and he finally returned to his room.

As my neck and back pain became known, I was informed that the hospital had a physical therapy department. I was surprised to learn that I could have an hour-long Thai massage to help alleviate my pain—for only $15! When I shared that wonderful news, my two sisters told me to hurry and make an appointment, with Catherine's offer to pick up the tab!

As Dr. Max prepared us for discharge, we listened carefully to every word he said. He was very clear that Darrell was prone to infection. He stressed that every item involved in the upcoming daily appointments had to be sterile. Dr. Max was so concerned that he suggested I take a digital picture of the wound every day for comparison. I was to watch closely for changes because the doctor's rotating hospital schedule would only allow him to see Darrell once a week.

When the day of Darrell's discharge came, I made my way downstairs to settle our bill. Thankfully, the hospital accepted credit cards, and thankfully we brought more than one! Dr. Bowen, being our Good Samaritan, drove us to several pharmacies so we could get some needed medical supplies. Then we went to Shari's house.

We were introduced to the kind lady and her cute little dog named Genevieve. Dr. Bowen grabbed our suitcases and carried them upstairs to the guest room. Shari showed us around her house, telling us to make ourselves at home. Inwardly, Darrell and I felt very emotional. After all the events over the past month, we were now being welcomed into a stranger's home—the home of a kind and compassionate stranger. We were very thankful for her hospitality but felt so undeserving. My husband's three-week recovery had officially begun.

The following day was our first of many trips to the ER. Darrell walked slowly and carefully climbed into Dr. Bowen's truck. The ride into Bangkok was roughly 35 minutes, sometimes longer depending on the traffic. On the drive, Dr. Bowen shared stories about his life and his current ministry with BEAMS (Bible Education and Missionary Service) Bibles. Our travel time together would have been a perfect opportunity to divulge the horrors we had faced in Eden, but we weren't ready to have a conversation of that magnitude so soon. For us, the story was still an unfinished tale of mixed feelings, horror and pain, not yet discussed even with each other. So for those sometimes-serious, sometimes-laughter-filled moments along the ride to and from the hospital, we allowed our own stressful story to slide to the back of our minds, and we enjoyed the details of his adventures and life's work.

The first visit to the ER went smoothly. A nurse took us to a small, curtained exam and treatment area within the ER. After the nurse removed Darrell's bandages, I took the first picture of his wound. Using a sterile "wound care kit," the nurse cleaned his incision and covered it with clean gauze and tape. Everything went well and surprisingly fast. I was pleased.

When we returned to Shari's house, we had our first visitor! Mrs. Jomhong came to visit, with a box full of goodies! She had soup, cookies, crackers, and many amazing tropical juices. We felt so incredibly loved.

I immediately felt comfortable asking Shari for one thing: I wanted to cook. I had been in hospitals for so long, I yearned to cook. On top of that, Darrell had lost so much weight that the sight of his frail frame nearly drove me to the kitchen. Thankfully, she was happy to allow me access. Not only did I whip up some of Darrell's favorite foods, but I think Shari enjoyed them, also. She was such a blessing to us, that I wanted to be a blessing to her, too.

On one particular trip to the ER, a young nurse had a question about the gauze that Dr. Max had given us. As a young, progressive doctor, he had used a newer, more expensive gauze than what she was used to working with. Since she was not familiar with how to properly use the gauze, she wanted to call him. With sterile gloves on her hands, she went into the open ER lobby, and I followed her. We were near the entrance where the wide automatic doors opened to allow patients on stretchers to enter the ER. Every day we saw patients come into the ER with open wounds, assorted injuries and infections. I watched our nurse as she picked up the phone to call Dr. Max. This phone was used by many people, including patients and their relatives. I was certain that her once-sterile gloves would have to be changed.

When she was finished, I followed close behind as she walked back to Darrell. As she was about to touch Darrell's wound, I stopped her by saying, "Wait, your gloves are not sterile anymore!" At that moment a problem arose when the hospital's international liaison intervened. The liaison was there to help us with the Thai-English language barrier. However, she strongly objected to my correction of the nurse. I quickly tried to explain that I had nearly lost my husband due to infection and that Dr. Max had instructed us to use only sterile supplies. However, before I could finish my sentence, the liaison stormed out of the room! Sadly, she went directly to Dr. and Mrs. Bowen whom she knew from their previous visits to the hospital and told them that if I corrected a nurse again, they would ask me to leave the hospital.

Not only was I deeply hurt that she had talked to them, but I was also stunned that she would not let me explain myself. After hearing only one side of the story, the Bowens were also unhappy with my correction of the nurse. We had not told anyone, including Dr. Max, what the first doctor in Eden had done. The liaison and our friends did not know Dr. Max had been very explicit explaining that everything needed to be sterile and that Darrell was extremely susceptible to infection.

The following day, I apologized to the nurse and the liaison. I explained that Darrell had already nearly died twice from infection and mentioned Dr. Max's specific instructions. I also decided to tell them about my mother's death, which explained my emotional state and why I was extremely protective of my husband. Thankfully, they understood and sympathized. In fact, they apologized to me, and the liaison even had tears in her eyes as she gave me a hug.

After each ER visit, Darrell spent the remainder of the day on Shari's sofa. (It was painful for him to make repeated trips up the stairs to our bedroom.) Because Darrell experienced more pain than expected, we asked Dr. Max to prescribe a different pain medication. However, after taking the new medicine, he was still experiencing inadequate relief.

I suddenly remembered that I had a large bottle of both pain medicine and muscle relaxers from the States! (I had them because my PA was certain I would experience serious back pain after so many long flights.) I quickly called Dr. Max and asked if Darrell could use the medication. After researching the brands, he prescribed that Darrell take them. Less than an hour after taking my medicines, Darrell's pain subsided completely, and he was finally able to relax.

Once again, we saw how God lovingly planned ahead for our time of need.

CHAPTER THIRTY

Two Steps Forward; One Step Back

OUR DAILY VISITS to the ER began to fall into a pattern. For a few days everything went smoothly. We were seen immediately, had the bandages changed, and went home quickly. However, the good days were interrupted by days where we encountered discouraging setbacks.

One such visit started off well. With no sick or wounded patients ahead of us, Darrell was seen right away. The nurse had him lie down, and she carefully removed the large outer bandage. When she removed the underlying gauze, we found that Darrell's colostomy base had leaked. I was filled with horror when I saw fecal matter on the stitches of his recently closed wound. I quickly turned away so Darrell would not see the tears that ran down my cheeks. As multiple nurses helped clean the contaminated wound, I let Dr. Bowen know there would be a delay. The nurses redressed the wound, documented the occurrence, and allowed us to leave.

Then one day, Dr. Max's recommendation to take daily pictures proved to be very important. As the nurse took off the bandages, he inspected the wound telling us, "Everything looks fine." Personally, I saw some redness on an area on Darrell's abdomen, which caught my attention.

I pointed to the area and asked the nurse, "What about this redness? Could this be a problem?"

The nurse reassured me that it was fine.

I quickly took a picture and compared it to the picture I had taken the previous day. As I viewed the two pictures back and forth, I could tell that there was indeed a new area of redness between rungs two and three of the retention sutures on the right side of the incision. I showed the nurse the two pictures, switching them back and forth. I pointed saying, "See, right here, between rung two and three of the retention sutures."

The nurse agreed with what I showed him on the camera, and he called for the doctor on call to check Darrell.

The doctor introduced himself and looked at Darrell's wound. He simply said, "He's fine."

Disappointed by this doctor's quick determination, I was compelled to say, "No doctor, please, look at the pictures."

After studying the pictures, the doctor agreed with my assessment about the change in skin color. He called for the surgeon on duty.

The surgeon walked into the room and introduced himself. He inspected Darrell's abdomen even longer than the others, but his conclusion was the same, that the wound was fine. I sighed deeply and spoke. "Please, Doctor, look at my pictures," I insisted, and I switched back and forth between the two photos.

After comparing the two pictures, the surgeon turned around and grabbed sterile gloves. He then asked the nurse for a scalpel from the sterile care kit. He slowly opened Darrell's incision and sure enough, there was infection. The surgeon then determined that Darrell's entire incision had to be opened, cleaned, and left open to close on its own. To Darrell's dismay, this procedure was done without anesthesia. As the surgeon cleaned the wound, Darrell grabbed the bed in obvious pain. I found it extremely difficult to see him in so much pain—again!

I was so emotional by what was happening that I had to leave the curtained area. I walked slowly toward Dr. Bowen, stopped directly in front of him, hung my head down and cried. I needed a few minutes to gather myself and explain why he had seen additional medical personnel gathering behind Darrell's curtained area.

On the way home from the hospital, we asked Dr. Bowen to gather some men from the church to anoint Darrell with oil, since his body continued to battle infection. Again, we were blessed to have four Godly men come to Shari's home and gather around Darrell. After their time of prayer, I took a picture of the men with Darrell.

Looking at that picture still brings me mixed emotions. Each time I look at it, I fondly remember the people who so graciously helped us in our critical time of need. However, I also recall how ill Darrell was as I gaze at his extremely thin face.

After a week of good appointments, we spotted another area of redness. Not taking any chances, the doctor opened part of the wound which had begun to heal to check for infection. This time, thankfully, they gave Darrell shots of local anesthesia. The shots administered to his belly were very uncomfortable for him. I am not sure why I chose to observe those invasive procedures because they were nearly as uncomfortable for me to watch. We were glad to hear the redness was nothing serious.

Amid the discouraging appointments, one day we received the best "medicine" ever. During a Skype call with our son, our grandson, Daniel, wanted to "talk" to us. After laughing at his toddler language that nobody understood, he blew kisses and made funny faces. Then, without warning, he said, "I love you" for the very first time, ever! We were tickled that he chose us as the first recipients of that phrase. I sometimes wonder if he somehow knew we needed to hear his wonderful words of love.

Above: The second anointing:
Dr. Bowen (seated next to Darrell); Tim Shook, who rushed us to the hospital, stands to his left; Pastor Bosje and Sakrapee Jomhong stand to his right.

Below: Our caring (and petite) nurses

CHAPTER THIRTY-ONE

Amazing Last Days in Thailand

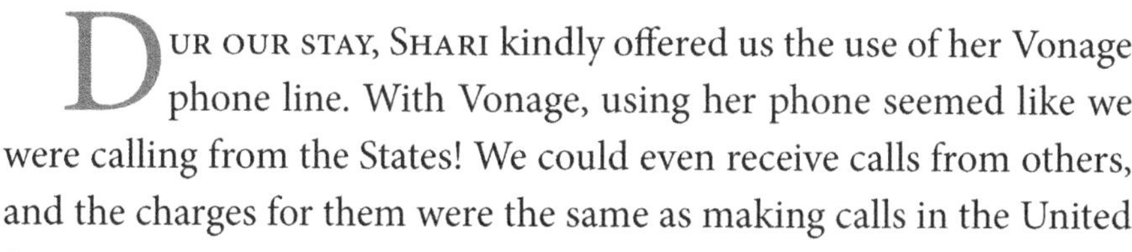

Dur our stay, Shari kindly offered us the use of her Vonage phone line. With Vonage, using her phone seemed like we were calling from the States! We could even receive calls from others, and the charges for them were the same as making calls in the United States.

Never dreaming when we left home that we would be gone for two months, and although I felt embarrassed, I realized I had to ask for help. Our dear neighbor, Rose, had been watching our home for us. We asked her to go through our mail one piece at a time, and open our bills so we could pay them on time. She also played our phone messages for us. We were quite helpless, and she was eager to assist, we were extremely grateful to have her support back home.

As Darrell's strength gradually returned, we were both able to engage in "everyday" activities once again, which we found to be very therapeutic—like cooking. I thoroughly enjoyed the liberty I had to cook. I made many of our favorites and discovered I make one of Shari's favorites too—Pavlova! This light and delicious fruit dessert originated in New Zealand, a country in which she once lived and served as a missionary. Considering her kindness to us, sharing her home and washing machine, etcetera, cooking for her was truly my pleasure!

We invited the Bowens for dinner as cooking a meal for them was the only "payment" they would allow. They would not let us pay for gas, despite the many trips to the hospital, the pharmacy, and the grocery store. He would not even take payment for the Coke Zeros he had bought for us at the hospital!

At some point we found out that McDonald's delivers in Thailand. When I learned this fact, I literally laughed out loud. When the laughter subsided, I called to place an order. Sure enough, in no time, a man arrived at Shari's house on a motorcycle—with McTherapy in hand.

Another meal-centered memory took place when the Bowens invited us to dinner one evening and served an American feast! They cared for us in so many ways but adding an amazing meal and a friendly game of dominos put them "over the top!" Darrell and I often found ourselves speechless by the genuine care we received from many missionary families serving in Thailand.

One day we invited Tim and Missy to dinner along with their two adorable children. We thoroughly enjoyed our evening together, sharing gifts for them that we brought from America. Their young son drew two pictures for us—one of Darrell and one of me. His drawings are precious…and humorous. When I look at his artistic rendition of my hair and feet, a smile comes across my face, and I seriously consider the need of a pedicure... or even a podiatrist!

After several days of recuperating at Shari's house, Darrell was strong enough to be left alone. I was excited to finally accomplish the task for which we had come to Asia—to share the Gospel with the people there. I joined the American missionaries, while another day I accompanied the Jomhongs and their Thai church. With the help of Thai translators, I was able to share the Gospel with about a dozen people. How thrilling it was for me to see the excitement in the eyes of those with whom I spoke when they learned they could be personally assured of Heaven.

Eventually Darrell felt strong enough to go to church services with the American missionaries. When he arrived, they brought a comfortable chair from the office for him to use in the auditorium; we enjoyed the service together. I was glad that Darrell was able to meet those phenomenal missionaries and to see the amazing work they had been doing in Thailand.

The following week I accompanied members of both churches for their organized time to share the Gospel. As Mrs. Jomhong drove me home, she somehow convinced me to sing in a trio at their church—*in Thai!* I tried my best to explain my inability to sing; however, the people there are much more interested in the spirit of one's heart than one's talent. While I sat in the passenger seat of her car, she told me the Thai words to "Amazing Grace," and I wrote them out phonetically. I thought it was interesting that she would pick that song, for it was grace that was showered upon us during our entire two-month trip!

When I returned to Shari's house, I told Darrell about the song and immediately went upstairs to the privacy of our bedroom to practice. Later that afternoon, Shari returned home from work. I was happy when Shari, who was successfully learning to speak the local language, asked if I was singing in my room in Thai. I was relieved that she did not think it was a different language!

The following morning, Darrell and I were eager to go to church. This time we would be attending Pastor Jomhong's church, where the entire service is in Thai—not English. I was surprised at how excited I was to sing, despite my lack of public singing experience and very little practice with the other two singers. When the service ended, Mrs. Jomhong asked me to come forward and stand at the front of the room. I stood there with tears in my eyes, as I was presented with roses by all the ladies and teen girls. One by one they came to me, gave me a rose, and thanked me for coming. Some ladies who only spoke Thai, smiled, and gently nodded. I can still hear Mrs. Jomhong's sweet words, "We love missionary!" What a great day; the service was wonderful, the singing went well, and we finished with a spectacular lunch.

As our departure grew nearer, the Jomhongs wanted to do a few special things for us. I was pleasantly surprised one day when Mrs.

Jomhong had her massage therapist come to the house. My back muscles were very tight, and I really needed to relax. I imagined I would receive a "Swedish" massage (primarily a gentle kneading of muscles) with the added uniqueness of using a translator. However, I was wrong.

To my surprise, the therapist proceeded to perform acupressure (with the emphasis on the word pressure!). Thai-style massage is completely different than Swedish-style massage. Thai massage involves a lot of bending and stretching techniques, as well as applying firm pressure to several areas on the limbs. While she worked on my feet, she pressed firmly on a particular area on my big toe. It hurt so badly that I almost came off the bed! When I screamed out in pain, she looked at me, paused, and pressed the same spot again. Once again, I felt a *sharp*, biting pain. I could not imagine why my toe would hurt that much!

I asked Mrs. Jomhong to have the therapist explain why my toe could possibly hurt that badly. After they spoke in Thai to each other, she told me it was the spot for "emotion." Wow! I might not understand acupressure, but I certainly went through some very emotional days—and my big toe certainly knew it!

One night the Jomhongs took us to a restaurant, but it was far from an ordinary restaurant. Located at the top of one of the tallest buildings in Bangkok, we rode a turbo-elevator to get there. After an amazing buffet of foods from around the world, we took a step outside on the narrow balcony. Not only were we taken aback by the breathtaking views of the city, but we were also standing among the clouds! It was truly magnificent! What a wonderful time we had exploring Bangkok with the Jomhongs.

Shari also wanted to take us to visit a special place outside of Bangkok. She drove us to the King's summer palace—the lovely retreat which was built by the King of Thailand in the 1600s and then updated in the latter 1800s. It is now only occasionally used for ceremonies and is open to the public year-round. Shari had said it was beautiful, but we had no idea exactly how beautiful it would be. The sculptured grounds and varied gardens, the ornate buildings, detailed fountains, and stunning carvings were spectacular! We rented a golf cart for Darrell so we could enjoy a self-guided tour. We were blessed with a gorgeous, sunny day and as we rode along, and we took pictures of the amazing sights. Toward the end of the tour, we rounded a pathway and saw a garden. As we got closer, we saw something else that nearly took our breath away.

Ahead was a lotus flower garden, a gorgeous (and famous) flower from Thailand. The flowers were in various stages of development—from bud to full bloom. The words "stunning" and "beautiful" do not do them justice. One in particular had random droplets of dew on its petals. The sun's light reflected from inside and behind the flower in such a way that it deeply affected Darrell. He told me that when he saw this flower, it was as if his eyes "drank the nectar" of its beauty. He said that it felt therapeutic, as if God had made it especially for him… almost a preview of Heaven's beauty and perfection. Needless to say, we each took several pictures of the wondrous lotus flowers.

From the palace, Shari drove us to a Thai attraction where I had an adventure of a lifetime. I rode an elephant! Because Darrell had been on one before and since he was not in any condition to ride, he took pictures and video for me. I was giddy as a schoolgirl and could hardly wait my turn! Climbing up the stairs to the platform, I became a little apprehensive as the large beast walked closer. He was huge!

Once I was seated, the "driver," who sat directly upon the elephant's neck, signaled, and immediately, my personal pachyderm started to walk. I was seated high upon its fabric-adorned back, complete with a royal seat and canopy. As he powerfully shifted his weight while walking, I held on tightly to the sides of the canopy. The amazing tour was surprisingly lengthy. After I climbed off my gentle giant, I excitedly ran down the steps to tell Darrell about my amazing experience.

Then we made another discovery…the owners of the elephants

also had a baby elephant! She was so incredibly cute that I squealed with delight! When I approached her to have my picture taken, she wrapped her adorable little trunk around my waist. I was completely overwhelmed with the delight of the experience!

After the hug of a lifetime, I took video of Darrell as he played with and teased the baby elephant* while he fed her some dried corn. That day was nothing short of spectacular!

The stunning lotus flower in bloom and in bud

---

*A video of Darrell with the baby elephant is posted on the book's website, www.withunwashedhands.com.

Above left: My fascinating ride; Right: Adorable baby elephant! Below right: Missionary Shari House, who allowed us to stay in her home; Left: a sweet girl I met on visitation

Abovet: The Boltons and the Jomhongs
Below:
Right: The Boltons at the king's summer palance
Left: Darrell at a Buddhist temple on vistation;
our last night in Thailand

C H A P T E R   T H I R T Y - T W O

An Eventful Flight Home

THE FINAL ERRAND before leaving Thailand was to make a pharmacy stop. We had to purchase sterile items for a bandage change during the flight home. As Dr. Bowen was forced to detour around many flooded roads, we saw the beginnings of the historic 2011 flood of Thailand.

We drove past many workers and volunteers filling sandbags, and Dr. Bowen shared with us that many of the people he would pick up to take to church lived in homes that had already been flooded. Many families lived at the water's edge and even over the canals in the area; they were called squatters. Most of them had no place to go—flood or no flood. They stayed in their homes until they were forced by even more dangerous conditions to leave. With water levels rising, the people in the homes by the canals were forced to stack pallets on top of each other, swim and climb to the top of them to sleep.

Little did we know that the flooding we saw would get much, much worse. With a third of the nation under six to twelve feet of water, Thailand would later call this flood "The Big One." Within weeks of our departure, our friends lost most of their possessions and were forced to evacuate their homes in the Bangkok area. We watched helplessly as they posted pictures of their beautiful homes surrounded by and filled with water. Our "Good Samaritan" would also lose the truck that he so graciously ministered to us with.

I spent our last night in Thailand busily packing our suitcases. I placed the sterile medical supplies and Darrell's colostomy items in our carry-on baggage. Since Darrell could not physically help me pack, he decided to go with Pastor Jomhong to share the Gospel. He had been too weak to join along for the past three and a half weeks, so he was very much looking forward to go.

They came across Buddhist temple grounds, where multiple buildings were situated in a park-like setting. They asked people if they had any questions about eternity. Many did! Darrell told me that his heart rejoiced to share the Gospel of Christ with the Thai people.

Packing our bags was like déjà vu. Here we were—about to take our much-longed-for flight home. Home to our own beds. Home to our precious family and friends. Home—such a precious word! Yet once again we had bittersweet feelings as we prepared for our journey. We found it difficult to say goodbye to those who had so generously given of themselves to help us—the wounded strangers in their midst. While we were excited to head home, we hated leaving the ones who had taken such good care of us, seeing us through some of the most trying times of our lives.

When we checked our luggage at the airport, again we had a suitcase that was overweight. I explained to the agent that the heavy one carried the entire set of CAT scan pictures, as well as two sets of medical folders and detailed hospital bills. One more time, grace was shown, and we were deeply thankful.

We were excited to be heading to Japan, the first leg of our flight home. Everything was going well when our trip suddenly took a jolting turn for the worse. When the flight attendant announced that we were about to make our descent, the gentleman one row behind us stood up to put his full-size laptop into the overhead bin. Somehow, it slipped from his hand and fell directly onto Darrell's abdomen! The sound of the fall was loud because the heavy laptop nicked the edge of Darrell's tray table. Thankfully, Darrell had a thin pillow resting on top of his belly. Darrell loudly exclaimed, "OH, MAN!!"

As the other passenger apologized profusely, I urgently asked Darrell, "Are you okay?!" To say that we were extremely concerned would be an understatement.

I pressed the call button, and the flight attendant came to our aid immediately. When he learned what had happened, he quickly made the infamous announcement on the airline's audio system, "Is there a doctor on the plane?" With the majority of the flight crew surrounding our seats, they asked if he was injured. I could not tell if any damage was done because without a sterile environment, we did not want to remove the tape and gauze from his wound. The captain called ahead to the airport in Japan, where priority wheelchair assistance was prepared to meet us when the plane landed.

Upon our landing, the chief flight attendant allowed Darrell to be the first passenger to deplane. An older Japanese gentleman met us and whisked my husband quickly through the airport. Although nothing was funny about the incident, I wonder how we must have appeared to onlookers: An older man racing through the airport, pushing a man in a wheelchair, with a tiny blonde lady sprinting unsuccessfully behind them, looking somewhat like a small baggage cart, desperately trying to balance three carry-on bags and a purse on her person!

Once we arrived at the airport's medical room, I had Darrell lie on the table for the bandage change. I was very nervous as I prepared the sterile supplies to remove the bandage. When I turned around to wash my hands, I was shocked to find their medical room had no soap. Unable to wash, I certainly would not treat Darrell's infection-prone wounds after sitting on a germ-filled plane! Instead, I looked closely at the taped gauze across his abdomen and did not see any sign of bleeding. I made the executive decision to avoid exposing his surgical site with dirty hands. I decided we would go directly to the Jacksonville Naval Air Station's hospital after landing in the States.

I checked Darrell's outer bandage repeatedly during the last two flights until we finally landed in Florida. Exhausted, we walked slowly off the plane and past security, where we were greeted by some of our faithful friends! Smiling and waving, they held a huge banner covered with handwritten notes from people from two *very special* churches. Tears flooded our eyes as we gazed upon familiar faces and a most incredible homecoming! Our friend, Dawn, generously offered to take us to the hospital, while Juan and Angie delivered our car and suitcases to our house.

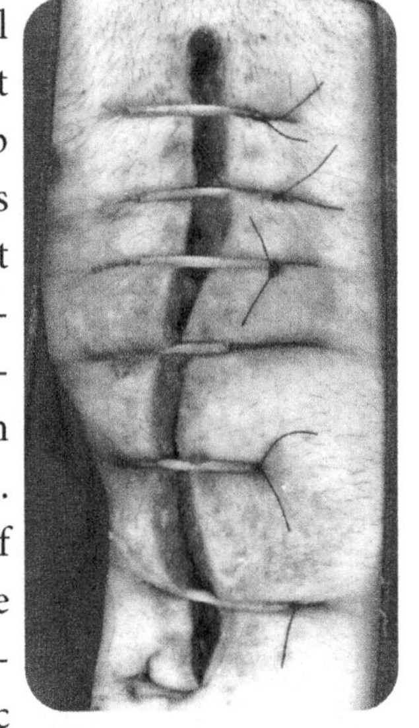

We arrived at the ER, where the hospital staff listened intently as we told them about Darrell's three surgeries *and* the recent laptop incident. As we finally removed the bandages in a sterile environment, we were relieved that no trauma was caused by the impact of the laptop on the plane. The surgeon at the base hospital told us that she had heard about retention sutures, but she had never actually seen them. In fact, she asked if Darrell wouldn't mind if hospital personnel could come to view the semi-open, S-curved incision. Adding a colostomy, healing wounds from the laparoscopic surgery and six cross-retention sutures, his abdomen, medically speaking, was impressive. We really should have kept count of the many medical personnel who came in the room to see the surgery site.

After Darrell was released, we headed home and were welcomed by another beautiful banner across our front door, which read "Home. Sweet Home!" That sign said it all! As we walked into our house, we were greeted with another surprise: Oreos®, Cheetos®, Tootsie Rolls®, M&Ms®, fruit, and a few homemade meals covered the island in our kitchen. With so many treats on the island, all I could do was laugh—a happy and *very* relieved laugh. No words could express the joy I felt to have my Darrell safe at home once again!

CHAPTER THIRTY-THREE

"What? Another Hospital?!"

WHAT AN AMAZING feeling it was to wake up in our own house! My husband prepared his famous home-roasted and freshly ground coffee, as he had done for most of our 30 years of marriage. Although a simple pleasure, it indicated to us that life was becoming more normal again.

Only 33 hours after returning to Florida, it was Sunday and time for us to go to church. Although a bit weary and worn, we were excited to thank everyone for their prayers and support. Darrell gave an inspiring testimony, in which he focused on the positive experiences. He explained that while many people going through trials ask, "Why me?" he chose to focus on God's faithfulness to us during the entire frightening and painful experience.

After church, we were grateful when our pastor invited us to his home to spend the afternoon with his family. Aside from the great meal, by visiting them we saved 40 minutes of drive-time each way between church services. We enjoyed our visit and a brief rest before the evening service.

Before church that evening, I changed Darrell's bandages. I noticed an unpleasant odor coming from the wound, and I knew immediately that something was wrong. I called Mary Jo without delay to ask her what we should do. She suggested we go back to the naval hospital where Darrell had already been seen. She also stressed to have them swab his wound for a culture.[1]

When Sunday evening services were over, we drove directly to the hospital. When we were informed that Darrell would have to wait a while, I drove through a nearby fast-food restaurant for dinner for us while he waited to be seen. After I returned, Darrell was finally called, and I went with him. I told the technician that our PA wanted Darrell's wound to be swabbed for a culture. The technician informed me there was no need for the culture. At my third request and repeated insistence, he reluctantly agreed. After a lengthy stay in the ER and with a fresh set of bandages, Darrell was released, and we drove home exhausted.

Several days of going through mail, catching up, and doing laundry, passed; then late one night I noticed that Darrell had a fever. Also, because of all the lifting I had done as we raced through Japan's airport, I was experiencing sharp back pains. Shortly before I changed Darrell's bandages, I took narcotic pain medicine and a muscle relaxer. By the time I noticed his fever, it was neither safe nor legal for me to drive him to the hospital. Since it was 10:30 p.m., I was afraid to call anyone for fear I would wake them up. I resorted to Facebook where I posted a message asking if someone local could take us to the ER. Dawn, our friend that took us to the hospital from the airport, was awake and happy to take us to the ER.

Because of the fever, the wound odor, and, most importantly, the fact that the culture had begun to grow, Darrell was admitted and immediately given an IV to administer antibiotics. With Darrell safe in their care at the naval hospital, Dawn took me home at 3:30 a.m.—after yet another long night at the ER. As I crawled into bed, I found it hard to believe that Darrell had been admitted to another hospital!

The following morning, I drove back to the hospital to be with him. Our day was spent observing nurses and medical students who came to see Darrell's unique and graphic wound, as well as the seldom-seen retention sutures. Suddenly, someone burst into the room holding the culture report. He explained that Darrell had two very dangerous and highly resistant bacteria—E. coli and Klebsiella pneumoniae.[2] Darrell quite possibly contracted the E. coli when his colostomy leaked on his stitches. I silently wondered if the second type of bacteria could have been from the doctor who repeatedly touched him without washing his hands.

The nurse immediately posted a sign on the door that Darrell's room was "contaminated." Anyone who entered our room was required to wear a gown and gloves and had to remove them outside our door when they left. The nurses were very concerned that the bacteria would enter his bloodstream. After a few hours of observation, it was determined that his wound was no longer tunneling, or in danger of spreading internally, the bacteria was confined to the outer surface of the skin. On a positive note, the doctor who treated Darrell was happy to remove half of his retention sutures. At this point, they were digging into his skin and causing him a fair amount of discomfort. He returned about a week later to have the remaining sutures removed. His physicians and caregivers decided to release Darrell because a spread of the dangerous, resistant bacteria could be deadly to others. The hospital staff worried for specific groups of their patients: the very young, the elderly, and especially those with a weakened immune system from illness or chemotherapy. When we heard Darrell was a literal danger to others, we left the hospital in almost disbelief. Our heads were spinning, and we felt like we were locked in a horrific story that refused to end.

We had Darrell's prescription for antibiotics filled, and I continued to change his bandages at home while he finished healing. In an extra bedroom, stacks of sterile supplies and saline were kept for my twice-a-day ritual. After several days I became a little more comfortable with my para-nursing duties.

One day, I donned the sterile gloves and changed his bandages and the colostomy base. Unfortunately, the adhesive did not seal properly and about an hour later, his colostomy bag began to leak. I had Darrell lie back down on the bed while I prepared the sterile supplies. I began to gently clean the adhesive from around the stoma.[3] I looked at the cotton ball and saw fresh blood. I quickly ran into the living room, buried my face in the sofa, and wept. I was devastated thinking that I had caused my husband additional pain. He had been through so much already, and now I had caused him to bleed. I honestly did not know what to do. When I stopped sobbing, I remembered Christy, a dear friend of ours who also had a colostomy. She was going through colon cancer treatment. In tears, I called her and told her what had happened. She immediately assured me that stomas bleed easily. When Christy continued that Darrell did not feel pain, despite the bleeding, I was exceedingly relieved! The stoma nurses in Eden and Thailand had failed to teach me this critical piece of information. After I gained my composure, I returned to Darrell and calmly replaced his colostomy base.

---

[1]*Culture*: a laboratory test to identify what type of bacteria may be present

[2]*Klebsiella pneumoniae*: a resistant bacteria found in the Far East

[3]*Stoma*: a surgical opening in the abdominal wall to allow the exposed intestine to expel waste

CHAPTER THIRTY-FOUR

The Fourth and Final Surgery

After three surgeries in third-nation countries, Darrell eagerly awaited his final surgery in Florida. I understood his desire to be rid of the colostomy, but he truly looked forward to the upcoming surgery. Possibly he looked forward with anticipation because this surgery would take place in an American hospital with familiar faces to visit him...and no language barrier. Everything about this surgery made him excited!

Darrell had endured the five months of having a colostomy with a great attitude, and everything went well. Christy, our friend who calmed me the night I saw blood, recommended her surgeon for Darrell's reversal[1] surgery. The surgeon, Dr. Fatemi, was a gentle man. Originally from Iran, he was very kind to us, and we were extremely comfortable with his performing the surgery.

The first time we met Dr. Fatemi, he took one look at Darrell's thin frame and said, "I will not do the reversal surgery until you are healthy again—maybe in four to seven months." That time frame would put surgery between the months of February to May the following year. He explained the complex and dangerous nature of this surgery compared to the one in Eden. He called the previous surgery, "damage control."

We told Dr. Fatemi that Dr. Max had suggested that Darrell's appendix be removed during the reversal surgery. If a problem ever arose with the appendix, it would be nearly impossible to remove it due to the excessive scar tissue in the area. Dr. Fatemi told us that it was not normal to remove the appendix during a reversal surgery. However, because we had requested the removal, he would attempt to remove the appendix—if he could find it. As we left that first appointment, I knew my job was to cook nutritious dinners to get Darrell healthy!

When we saw Dr. Fatemi the following month, he was pleasantly surprised! Darrell had his color back, and he was at a much healthier weight. We were shocked to hear him say he could perform surgery the following month—November! Because our second grandson was due to be born in December, we chose to postpone the surgery until January. Each appointment with Dr. Fatemi made us more pleased that he was our surgeon.

We scheduled Darrell's surgery for January 13th. Darrell was busy throughout the week of the surgery with the required pre-operative procedures. We were relieved when our medical bills in the States amounted to only our small co-pay with our Tricare insurance. We were still trying to recover from the excessive bills we had accumulated overseas.

Darrell had spent an abundance of time organizing and making copies of our medical records and the stacks of hospital bills. When we mailed the heavy envelope to Tricare, we prayed for mercy because legally they were not required to cover any of the medical expenses we had previously paid.

Weeks later, we received a letter from them. With hearts pounding, we sat together on the sofa to open it. We expected nothing—especially after reading their coverage requirements. However, we were extremely surprised that they had overlooked the legality of the matter and had sent us a check! Although we did not receive the full reimbursement, we knew God had once again answered our prayers!

When Darrell's "big day" arrived, our pastor and a friend from church stayed with me during the surgery. Having company we knew and loved in the waiting room was comforting. The surgery lasted longer than expected, but eventually Dr. Fatemi entered the waiting room to talk to us. I expected to hear, "Everything went great!" However, that was not the case.

Dr. Fatemi said, "Darrell is in recovery and doing fine, but the surgery was very, very difficult. I did find his appendix, so I was able to remove it. I also repaired three hernias, but without mesh because of the combined surgery on the colon. There was very little tissue to work with, so the joining was not perfect. We need to hope and pray that it stays joined together."

I tried not to show my disappointment at the potential for a very serious complication. I remember seeing the look on Pastor Hall's face; he was apparently as shocked at the update as I was. Pastor and I were both very quiet after Dr. Fatemi walked away. Neither of us quite knew what to say.

I made phone calls to our family members to let them know that Darrell was in recovery. I also explained the area of concern the doctor had shared. I did not take lightly the ease of simply using my cell phone to speak to loved ones. I was thankful for many conveniences we had, unlike the surgeries overseas. Lastly, I updated my Facebook status and explained the surgery results and the specific matter for which to pray.

Something had concerned me ever since I saw Darrell's colon on the tray in Eden. The entire specimen was very thick with huge multicolored bubbles. There was no visible thinning down to its normal size, nor was there any hint of the healthy pink color on the ends. I could only surmise that unhealthy tissue had remained inside Darrell's abdomen. I had repeatedly explained my concerns to the first doctor in Eden, but he had never answered my question or addressed what I had observed.

I asked Dr. Fatemi after the reversal surgery if any unhealthy tissue remained. He articulated my fears as he said, "Yes," and explained that after he had removed the unhealthy tissue, the reconnection had to be made much closer to the rectum. "Because of removing so much tissue, the joining was not as optimal as I had hoped."

I was disappointed that the concerns I had harbored since August were indeed founded. I began to pray earnestly for the surgical connection to be secure. If the connection leaked, the consequences could be fatal.

During one of our last appointments before surgery, Dr. Fatemi warned us, "God forbid it should ever come apart." As the memory of those terrifying words rang in our ears, we began to share with others how they could specifically pray for my husband's healing.

Darrell teasingly called it, "Seal and heal."

As we settled into yet another hospital room, we were happy that the final chapter in our story was about to come to an end. Thankfully, each day in the hospital brought Darrell a little more strength and many wonderful visitors. One couple, precious friends from Indiana, happened to be in Florida and made time in their schedule to stop by the hospital. We were thrilled they had come to see us, sweetly bringing gifts—including McTherapy! Our friends had driven six hours out of their way while on vacation to see Darrell! Many local friends who had encouraged us during our two-month ordeal also came to the hospital. Their visits meant more to us than we could ever adequately express.

Darrell and I discussed how encouraging it was that others gave up some of their time to visit. We remembered what it had felt like being alone and hurting in the overseas hospitals, and we did not take these visits for granted. We decided we wanted to be the "Wayne and Louise" or the "Dr. Bowen" for others. We do not want to only receive those blessings, but we sincerely want to pass them along to others.

Ironically and unintentionally, our friend Christy and Darrell had scheduled their reversal surgeries within a few days of each other and in the same hospital! She was recovering from her surgery around the corner on the same floor. Delighted with the timing of their surgeries, we took turns visiting each other.

The evening before Darrell's discharge date, he began to run a fever. By morning it had reached 100°. The doctor decided to keep him another night to monitor his condition. I had a restless mind because of his fever, and I did not sleep much that night.

Dr. Fatemi came by our room to explain how to care for the wound where Darrell's stoma had been. We learned that after his surgery, his deep wound had not been stitched closed. Instead, it would have to heal on its own from the inside out.

When the original gauze from the surgery was removed, it came out in one very, very long strip, reminding me of the magic trick done with handkerchiefs! By the time all the gauze had been removed from the wound, I was laughing! How Dr. Fatemi fit all that gauze inside the surgical site, I will never know! As he placed new sterile gauze, moistened with saline, into the gaping wound, he told me I would have to perform the same procedure daily. He explained that the wet gauze would later dry. When removed, it would gently *tug* the surrounding tissue which would promote healing. He made the packing of the deep wound look so easy.

I soon discovered packing the surgery site was not easy at all, especially when Darrell was home and not on IV pain medication anymore! As I gently pushed the gauze inside his open wound with my gloved fingers, I purposely looked away as he winced. While I performed these difficult duties, I pondered how wonderfully important it was for me to be so medically minded. It took many weeks for his wound to close, bringing us both great joy when a small, folded piece of gauze, taped down over the wound meant we were finished.

I experienced even greater joy the day I could finally remove the stacks of sterile supplies from the spare bedroom.

---

[1]*Reversal*: a surgery reattaching previously separated intestines to eliminate the need of a colostomy

CHAPTER THIRTY-FIVE

Wounded, but Still in Action!

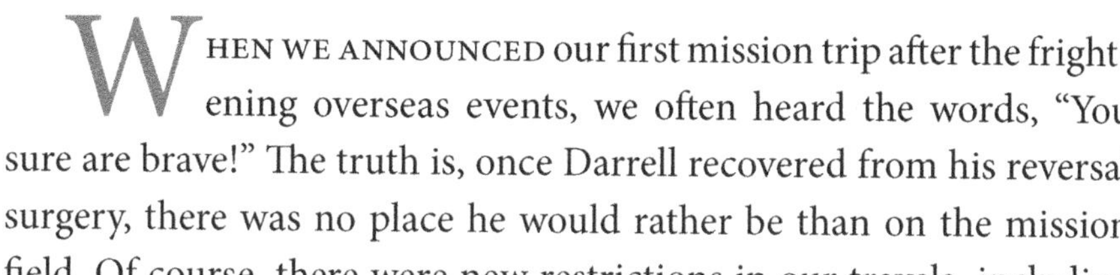

WHEN WE ANNOUNCED our first mission trip after the frightening overseas events, we often heard the words, "You sure are brave!" The truth is, once Darrell recovered from his reversal surgery, there was no place he would rather be than on the mission field. Of course, there were new restrictions in our travels, including lifting limitations for both of us. Darrell's multiple surgeries have left him with a *lifelong* lifting limitation of only ten pounds. Nevertheless, his desire to work with missionaries had not waned, not one bit!

Both Dr. Max and Dr. Fatemi were correct in saying that Darrell was susceptible to hernias. Not long after his final surgery to close the stoma, the unmeshed repairs to his three hernias gave way. Since Darrell's reversal surgery in January of 2012, his tummy has bulged out more than four inches.

Despite being forced to wear an abdominal belt, he looks and feels great! He also sports an impressive scar on his abdomen, which serves as a permanent reminder of his experiences—not only of the abuse his body endured, but also of the amazing miracles that God performed as He saved Darrell's life.

I believe God spared my husband's life for many reasons. God, in His absolute power and mercy, allowed me to keep my husband of 30 years. His same mercy allowed our children to keep their father and will give our grandchildren the opportunity to love and learn from their Papa. When considering his mother, his siblings, and all the friends who would have missed his caring and uplifting ways, one realizes these are more than enough reasons for God to have decided to spare his life.

But aside from the personal relationships he enjoys, it is evident that God also had His own thoughts about Darrell. I have observed that God has used these events in Eden to give Darrell even more power and boldness when he steps behind a podium to speak. I have always enjoyed the opportunity to hear Darrell speak. However, since God intervened and spared his life, I see more than my husband speaking. I see a messenger whose life has been carefully preserved so that he can continue to work wherever his Heavenly Father will lead.

Our last several mission trips have been remarkable! I have silently watched men and women approach Darrell with tears in their eyes, sincerely expressing how much his words meant to them. We have received many heartfelt letters and emails of thanks since our experience, and the Lord has used these to encourage us and reconfirm our commitment to this ministry—for as long as our health and funds permit.

Darrell and I love sharing the story of what befell us overseas—not because *we* did anything spectacular—but because we can now testify what *the mighty power of God* did for us when we were in that very desperate situation. Others hearing the details of these events has brought about an even greater response than we ever imagined. We often hear comments like, "Your story has increased my faith!" As God so graciously cared for us and miraculously spared Darrell's life, *our* personal faith has grown. Imagining that what transpired could help *another person's* faith never came to our minds. Darrell and I understood that we could not simply *enjoy* the benefit of experiencing the healing hand of God and do nothing about it; we feel we would be terribly irresponsible if we did not share our story.

Since Darrell's recovery from his reversal surgery, we have traveled to 14 countries—Myanmar (Burma), Ghana, Tanzania (twice), Jamaica, India, Thailand (three times) Qatar, Ireland, Japan, Cambodia, Vietnam, Kenya, Guam, and Honduras, as well as many trips to several different islands in the Philippines. The Lord has used Darrell to reach many more people with the Gospel message; and by His grace, we look forward to many more opportunities in the future!

My main desire in writing this book is for the reader to understand this important thought: God is always trustworthy, and we should never lose hope in His continued help! Our hope in the Lord was our focus during our entire ordeal. He was also our strength.

My hope is to encourage others to bear one another's burdens as Galatians 6:2 exhorts. Selfless people brought this wonderful passage to life during our trial which truly helped sustain us.

I could not write this book, sharing with you the miracles we experienced, without properly introducing you to the God Who met our every need. Many people know Who Jesus is; however, knowing Who He is and trusting Him for salvation are very different. Jesus said, *"I am the way, the truth, and the life: no man cometh unto the Father, but by me"* (John 14:6).

Going to Heaven someday is not determined by our religion or our good deeds. Instead, our salvation is entirely based on having faith. *"For by grace are ye saved through faith; and that not of yourselves: it is the gift of God: Not of works, lest any man should boast"* (Ephesians 2:8, 9). Salvation is turning from our sin, and putting our faith in Jesus. Truly it is that simple. The Bible says we have all sinned. Honestly, we know this in our own hearts. I often tell people that I do not have to teach my grandchildren to tell a lie or to fight, this comes naturally to all of us. Sin separates us from God, which means ultimately an eternity in Hell.

In this hopeless condition, each one of us needs a Savior, and God lovingly provided One when He allowed His very own Son to die on the Cross. In doing so, Jesus paid the penalty for every sin mankind has ever committed. Jesus' payment is God's gift to each of us; all we have to do is accept God's amazing, free gift of salvation. The Bible tells us *"For whosoever shall call upon the name of the Lord shall be saved"* (Romans 10:13). Whosoever means that anybody can call for that help. Our skin color, gender, or financial status does not matter; if we simply call upon Him, He *will* save us. That is a promise from God!

To call upon God for salvation simply means "praying, speaking from *your* heart *to* God in Heaven." It truly is amazing that God hears us whenever we pray—whether we are in a church, on a balcony in Eden, or quietly reading a book.

You may want to ask God right now to forgive your sins and save you, but perhaps you are not sure what to say. I will add a simple prayer that you can say in your own words and heart. Remember, God cares much more about *the sincerity of our heart* than the exact words we may say in a prayer. When you do pray and mean it within your heart, the Lord *promises* He will save you!

> *"Dear Heavenly Father, I believe that Your Son, Jesus, died on the Cross for me. I know I have sinned, and I am sorry. Please come into my heart and forgive me of my sins and help me to forsake them. The best I know how, I receive Jesus right now as my personal Savior. Thank You for saving me and for giving me eternal life. Please help me to live for You. In Jesus' name I pray, Amen."*

If you prayed this prayer from your heart and asked the Lord to save you, Darrell and I would love to hear that wonderful news! If even one person were to trust Jesus as their personal Savior, then writing this book was worth every tear-filled emotion or hour spent on it! Please email us at: withunwashedhands@gmail.com

CHAPTER THIRTY-SIX

We're Baaack... Seven Years Later

As time went on, we recognized that an unsettling comment by Dr. Fatemi was becoming reality. The 2012 sutúre-repaired hernias began to give away, and my husband was left with a shocking abdominal deformity. I was impressed that Darrell never complained about his bulging hernias or the support band he was forced to wear at all times—even in the extreme heat of some of our missionary journeys in countries such as the Philippines, Qatar, and Africa.

Darrell would need another surgery, but not for vain or superficial reasons. He lived each day with unprotected intestines, increasing the chance of an intestinal blockage or strangulation, which can cause intestinal tissue death. In addition, he faced the ever-present risk of injury if something hit his abdomen. I have added a picture of his abdomen, not to shock or disgust, but to reveal his reality. Darrell's condition did not stop him from serving in our ministry. In fact, pastors in the Philippines requested Darrell reveal his intense-looking abdomen to the men in their church. The sight provided a reminder to pray for missionaries serving in unfriendly territories.

When we had a break from our travels, we made an appointment with a hernia specialist. Within moments of examining Darrell's abdomen, the doctor said, "This is not a hernia repair; you will need an abdominal reconstruction." *An abdominal reconstruction?!* We never knew such an intense sounding surgery even existed.

The doctor emphatically recommended one particular specialist—Dr. Walker. Excitedly, we made our way to the appointment to meet this highly recommended surgeon. Dr. Walker confirmed that Darrell would need the reconstruction, a complex and dangerous surgery to repair the three bulging hernias. He explained to us that Darrell would experience significant pain; however, his goal was to improve Darrell's quality of life, increase his lifting limit, and more importantly, protect those intestines!

Darrell was in great spirits the morning of the surgery, and although my faith was strong, I couldn't help feeling somewhat emotional, remembering his previous overseas surgeries. We were surrounded by our dear friend, Juan Cardona, and our pastor, Raymond Hall, and his wife Lisa, who prayed with us and encouraged us.

The surgery would take most of the day, and the hospital staff assured me they would call with surgical updates throughout the day, beginning with the "first-cut" notification.

After the surgical team whisked Darrell away for surgery, the four of us went to an early lunch. What a wonderful distraction! I couldn't believe how long it took for someone to call with the first-cut notification. Finally, after we had finished eating, I received the phone call that surgery had begun. The nurse also mentioned that the doctor was still determining what mesh to use, which I found to be a bit odd.

Once Darrell was settled in surgery, Pastor and Lisa prayed with me again and headed home. Juan and I waited together for many hours, silently praying with little-to-no news from the medical staff.

Around four o'clock, a very tired Dr. Walker entered the waiting room. In fact, he looked like he had been in a grueling fight. Dr. Walker asked in a frustrated tone, "Who did his last surgery?!"

Shocked by his emphatic question, I replied, "His reversal surgery?" I motioned with my hand to the area where a colostomy bag would go.

He exclaimed, "No! This!" As he dramatically moved his hand up and down the abdominal area where Darrell's long incision was, I finally understood his question.

"The doctor in Eden," I answered. At our initial visit with Dr. Walker, I had made a remark about the anti-American doctor who tried to kill Darrell. Dr. Walker didn't realize until he was in the midst of surgery how accurate my comment was.

Dr. Walker proceeded to provide information about the surgery. He explained that when they opened Darrell's abdomen, the medical team stared in disbelief. They found large staples and clips throughout his intestines. The stunned doctor had to revise his surgical plan, using a completely different kind of mesh. The nurse's delayed notice of the first cut and additional mesh comment now made perfect sense.

I had one grave concern leading up to surgery. Darrell's hernias were so large and protruding that his skin was extremely tight. I could not imagine Dr. Walker being able to cut open his abdomen without inadvertently slicing into his intestines. Dr. Walker confirmed my suspicion, explaining that they did nick his bowel in a couple of places but were able to repair them successfully.

Dr. Walker said the surgery was a success, then he continued to explain that Darrell would be in recovery for about an hour and then transported to his room. After waiting nearly two hours, I walked to the nurses' station to get an update. The nurse made a phone call and told me that Darrell was experiencing severe pain in recovery. The medical staff had to call the anesthesiologist to return.

My heart instantly broke. About 9:00 p.m., the medical staff finally wheeled my exhausted husband into the room. After quick, happy greetings from our friends, everyone went home to give Darrell the rest that he desperately needed.

The following morning Juan and I returned to the hospital. Juan wanted to see Darrell before leaving to go home to St. Augustine. Shortly after he left, Darrell experienced a frightening complication. He began to look ashen-gray, and his blood pressure began to plummet as his heart rate soared. Multiple alarms sounded, and instantly, medical personnel flooded into the room, followed by Dr. Walker. I watched Darrell's BP fall to 51/37, and his heart rate rise to 140. Fear gripped my heart.

I had communicated Darrell's falling BP statistics to his sister Diane and our pastor, who is also a licensed paramedic. What I did not know was that Raymond and Lisa were at the hospital to make another visit, and with each new update, he told Lisa that he thought Darrell was going to have to return to surgery.

When Darrell became dizzy, a nurse put smelling salts under his nose, saying, "Darrell, stay with us!"

I began to shake in fear when suddenly Raymond and Lisa walked into the room. As they came over to comfort me, Raymond peeked at Darrell's monitor, confirming that his situation was indeed serious.

The medical staff performed an EKG and drew blood, ordering immediate results. Darrell's drain tubes filled much too quickly with blood, which Dr. Walker attributed to possible internal bleeding. He immediately ordered a bolus[1] of increased IV fluids and four units of blood, which helped tremendously. Dr. Walker only wanted to perform surgery as the last resort.

Thankfully, the Lord intervened after much prayer was offered on Darrell's behalf, and the medical team finally brought the bleeding under control. Darrell later told me the episode was the closest he had felt to his weakened state in Eden.

The next five days were extremely difficult for Darrell. The pressure in his abdomen was so tight that he could barely sip water, and he certainly could not eat. He needed help to walk, often with a nurse on each side, as he was extremely shaky. Seeing my once strapping husband so weak was painful for me to endure. In fact, he only got out of the canary-yellow socks, which were reserved for their fall-risk patients, as he was about to be discharged.

Nearly a week after surgery, Darrell was able to have a light diet.

While he was fasting, all I did was eat for stress therapy. I was glad our hospital room did not have a scale!

We had an incredible staff of caring nurses and a very attentive doctor. At the time of the surgery, our book (without these two new chapters) was already in print, and I shared copies with our doctor and nursing staff. One nurse finished reading the book before her next shift, exclaiming what a miracle Darrell was.

Our feelings mirrored those from our time in Eden and Thailand as Darrell's discharge from the Viera Hospital were once again bittersweet.

Dr. Walker was right. After his full recovery, Darrell was able to resume his prior lifting capabilities. Finding luggage handlers overseas was often difficult—if not impossible. Consequently, Darrell's increased lifting capability was extremely important for our continued travel.

As much as I want to say our story ends here, I simply cannot.

---

[1]*bolus*: a quantity of fluid or medicine given intravenously at a controlled, rapid rate.

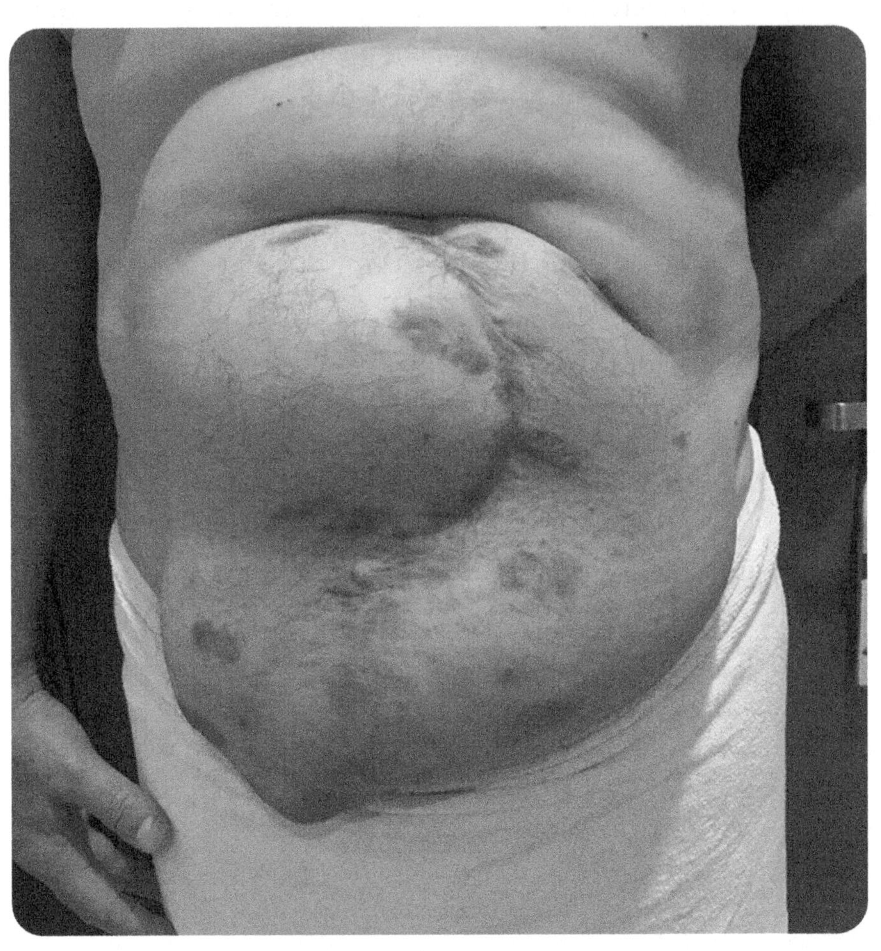

Darrell's abdomen before reconstructive surgery

CHAPTER THIRTY-SEVEN

Re-Reconstruction

After Darrell's painful abdominal reconstruction, things were going rather well. Darrell enjoyed regaining the ability to lift again, and our ministry was busier than ever. We took our annual trip to see our six grandkids and extended family in California.

However, it did not take long before we started to see subtle changes in Darrell's abdomen. He became more careful with lifting and exercise so as not to put pressure on his core muscles. Despite his caution, his hernias continued to grow.

Parts of this book were difficult to write, including losing my mother and missing her funeral, watching my husband hover near death's door, and experiencing the uncertainty of Darrell's extremely painful reconstruction surgery. However, the new abdominal breech left me feeling deep sadness, affecting us in a tender way.

In Darrell's first multiple-hernia condition, the hernias protruded outward. His abdomen certainly looked drastic, but it did not disrupt his life. Everything remained relatively normal, except for his concern for intestinal injury or that his wider profile might stay forever. This hernia was different though. His small intestines no longer protruded outward, they were hanging low, so low that they hung over his groin area.

My heart literally ached to see how this particular hernia affected my husband both emotionally and physically. I reassured him many times that his body carried battle scars of incredible proportions; his body was *not* defective. Instead, I considered him a walking, talking miracle! In my eyes, his body did not appear as he saw it. In fact, since he never used his limitations and deformity to stay home and enjoy his retirement years, but rather chose to serve God faithfully, he entered into "hero" status in my mind. Even now, tears fall as I type this chapter, knowing the many times he felt unattractive or the times the weight of the hernia didn't allow his body to function as he wanted.

When we married, we said we would love each other through sickness and in health, for better or for worse. Although it appeared we were experiencing the "worse," our marriage did not hinge on the abilities or disabilities of our bodies. I want to be discreet, but I must share how much that man has suffered and endured. Because the hernias began to affect our intimacy, we knew it was time to make another appointment with Dr. Walker.

Darrell and I enjoyed every appointment with Dr. Walker. He is a pleasant and engaging person and an excellent doctor. After chatting about our recent mission trips, Dr. Walker looked at Darrell's failed reconstruction. He was disappointed to see how drastic it was, and we were saddened to hear that repairing the hernia was out of his ability. He told us plainly that he would only trust one doctor, Dr. Carbonell in Greenville, South Carolina, with his most unique patient—my husband.

South Carolina?! My immediate thought was that we would not have our much-loved pastor and wife there or the many friends who came to visit and encourage us during Darrell's first reconstruction near our Florida home.

Once our insurance approved the out-of-state surgery, we made an appointment to meet the surgical team. In a wonderful way of provision, some dear Florida friends introduced us to a sweet widow who housed us during our stay. Heading to an appointment in a foreign city and preparing for the sixth surgery since our tragic story began was surreal.

Once there, I was horrified to see Dr. Carbonell and two of his assistants aggressively push on Darrell's hernias, but they needed to feel exactly where the breeches were that allowed the intestines to hang as they did.

During Darrell's hospital stays in Eden and Thailand (except for his two days in ICU) and the reversal surgery, I had slept in his room. The doctor ordered a CT scan to assist their preparation, and by the time surgery was scheduled for fall of 2020, Covid-19 was already a worldwide pandemic. However, the Greenville hospital held firm to the Covid rules, and I was only permitted to see him for a brief, allotted four-hour period of time.

This surgery was reminiscent of Darrell's colostomy reversal. Darrell was excited at the prospect of having his abdomen repaired. *Me?* Not so much. I almost lost him in 2011, and he had suffered so much during his first abdominal reconstruction in 2018. Reliving the emotions of the ordeal was daunting, especially considering the danger of the coronavirus.

In the moments before surgery, Dr. Carbonell asked Darrell if he was particularly attached to his belly button. The doctor continued to explain that his surgical plan would require its complete removal. We had to laugh because Darrell had lived 50 years with the original one. After the surgeries in Eden and Thailand, it had been placed a bit higher, and after the abdominal reconstruction, it had shifted to the right! Considering the numerous relocations of his belly button, Darrell smiled and said, "Go ahead, take it."

The surgery lasted several hours, and Covid prevented anyone from sitting with me. I was driven, quite literally, to get French-fry McTherapy to keep me distracted. Our dear nurse-friend, Donna, offered to be on a video call when the doctor came to update me after surgery. Because my emotions were heightened, I welcomed not only a second set of ears, but ones with extensive medical knowledge. Dr. Carbonell had no problem with Donna listening to his post-surgery update, although he was rather blunt in describing how Darrell's low-hanging intestines were before the surgery. He must have imagined that Donna, being a nurse, had "heard it all." He told us that the surgery went well, and that he was able to place a large, solid piece of mesh to hold everything in place. He said, "Darrell will feel *extremely tight* for a while."

The doctor used a different form of post-surgical pain control without narcotics. They administered a nerve block due to the extensiveness of the surgery. Without the narcotics, Darrell didn't have the usual post-surgical drug-like feeling. He actually recovered very well, and he was able to leave the hospital after only a few days! What a difference that was from his first abdominal reconstruction!

During the short post-surgical hospital stay, I was concerned when they allowed Darrell to have solid food immediately, including chicken and broccoli! A few days after Darrell's release, he was very uncomfortable and felt pressure in his abdominal area. Taking a close look, I noticed there was some swelling in his abdomen. Alarmed, I sent pictures to Donna, who recommended we start measuring his waist regularly.

When Darrell began to feel worse and gained an entire inch in an hour's time, we rushed him to the ER. The attending doctor ordered a CT scan, which showed that Darrell had an intestinal blockage. Once he was admitted, he was given a nasogastric tube (NG tube)[1] to help relieve the pressure. One of his nurses agreed with me that Darrell should not have eaten solid food after such an extensive abdominal surgery, especially broccoli. Going from the excitement of an early hospital release to a week-long readmission was disheartening. Darrell disliked the NG tube as would be expected, exclaiming, "I know what NG stands for: not good!"

After his release from the hospital and a two-week recovery in Greenville, the doctor allowed him to make the drive home and cleared him to do the driving himself! Darrell has since made a complete recovery and has regained his full lifting capabilities. As I finished this chapter, we were serving in Guam for three months, filling the pulpit for a missionary family on furlough. We are also making plans to serve for six months in Thailand later this year. Our prayer (and we hope you will join us in this prayer) is that this is the final chapter of our dramatic medical story. However, our desire is to continue our ministry story and serve others for many years to come.

Darrell is not only a true gentleman; he is a warrior, an exceptional speaker, a tremendous role model, and without question, a hero.

---

[1]nasogastric tube (NG tube): A tube used for suctioning stomach contents, inserted through the nose and down the esophagus into the stomach.

One Final Thought

ONE FINAL THOUGHT as I contemplate the traumatic and painful events we endured, and the remarkable way God cared for us. Now that the many pieces of the medical puzzle have been made clear, we can properly answer the doctor's questions about Darrell's being "Superman." I long for the day when Darrell and I can return to Eden. One of the first places I would want to go is to the hospital to find that doctor. My only desire would be to make him aware that it was neither Darrell nor training by the U.S. military that kept him alive. Instead, I would introduce him to the One who spared his life and share how he too can be assured of Heaven.

Bitterness imprisons life; love releases it.
–Harry Emerson Fosdick

MVP Missions' Ministry

WE LOVE OUR ministry! We are honored to be able to travel and work with others around the world. Thankfully, God is willing to use those who make themselves available, a willing vessel is what He seeks to use. We have begun to pulpit fill for missionaries as they need to leave their ministry and return to the states due to medical needs or furlough. Our ministry conducts many children's feedings, as well as shipping good quality Bibles overseas.

If you are interested in hearing more about our ministry or to see our presentation, please email us. We would be happy to hear from you. Email mvpmissionaries@gmail.com

Our background is grounded on the fundamental teaching of the King James Bible and the teachings of the Baptist church. We keep things simple on our mission trips. We use the Bible as our authority, we teach and preach salvation by faith in Jesus Christ alone, and we direct people to their local church for further growth in the Christian life.

The following are some encouraging notes about our ministry:

DARRELL AND JOANIE Bolton were a great blessing to our ministry here in Ghana. The two of them are such a wonderful couple and a complement to each other, but most of all they have a huge heart for people—both to the missionaries and the native people. Bro. Bolton's preaching was an inspiration to our church, and Mrs. Bolton has a very infectious spirit that is one of a kind. Both of them obviously walk with God and have a special place in His heart. It was a great encouragement to have them with us, and we look forward to their return.

– Pastor Ted Speer, *Missionary*
Ghana, West Africa

How can we ever thank you enough for the personal sacrifice you have made to come and visit us? I love my life and the privilege of serving God in Ghana, but there are many days the Devil whispers in my ear to quit. Sometimes I'm tempted to agree with the Devil, and it's at those times when God does something special for me. Your visit is that "special something" that God has done for me. It has been the encouragement that I needed in so many different ways. I wish that more pastors in America understood the importance of your ministry to missionaries on the field. I will be forever grateful for the "ministering" you have done to our little family. We love you so much! Thanks again.

– Lindsey Osgood, *Missionary*
Ghana, West Africa

Thank you so much for coming to Ghana to spend some time with our family. You were a HUGE encouragement to us! Thank you for all the gifts you gave us. You are so generous. I have really enjoyed reading the book I got about the life of David. Bro. Bolton, I really enjoyed seeing you conduct services in the area schools we went to. I got a lot of ideas for our ministry to start using more visuals in our work with children.

Sometimes as we missionaries are busy ministering to others, we need someone to minister to us, and that is exactly what you have done for us. You have literally served us while you were here. With words, I can't say a big enough "thank you," but I want you to know your labor made a great impact on our lives.

I love you and pray that God will continue to use you to encourage His servants around the world for many years to come.

– Charles Osgood, *Missionary*
Ghana, West Africa

Thank you so much for coming! It was a bigger sacrifice than you expected, and you handled it splendidly! Your attitude through the illness, surgery, and your mother's death were your greatest ministry to all of us; I know we and our people will never forget you! It was an absolute JOY to get to know you both so well! We will miss you! Please come again and let us serve you again as unto the Lord!

– "Wayne" & "Louise"
Missionaries to "Eden"

As I just wanted to let you know how much of a blessing your ministry is to missionaries like myself. For the past eighteen years that I have served on the field, my parents have only been able to visit three times for a total of eight weeks. No other family members have been able to make the journey. People such as yourself who make the effort to travel to different mission fields to serve not only the churches but also the missionaries are truly a blessing.

During your hour of need in Thailand, the Lord chose to let our paths cross for several weeks. It was a blessing to have you in my home and to get to know you both and to see your love for the Lord, for missions, and especially for missionaries. Even in that difficult time, I saw you let the Lord use you to be a blessing to others. I thank the Lord that we met, that we are friends, and that I know one day again, you will return to share in the burden, lighten the load even if just for a few days, and encourage this missionary's heart. My love to you both.

– Shari House, *Missionary*
Nigeria, New Zealand, and Thailand

I TRULY APPRECIATE the spirit Bro. and Mrs. Bolton bring to the field. They do not hesitate to jump right in and help with all of our activities. They love to be a part of everything! And they are not deterred by the long hours and excruciating heat. We are always refreshed by their optimistic outlook and positive attitude. On a personal note, I just want to express my gratitude for the Boltons. They have invested in our ministry here since the very beginning. They have encouraged and helped us on both sides of the ocean. Only a missionary can understand what it means to have a visit from folks from home. And the Boltons go out of their way to make that visit special, my heart is always touched by their thoughtfulness. The positive conversation and wholesome laughter is a big help. I'm excited about the future of our friendship and the visits the Boltons will make to the Philippines. Thank you for being willing to go. We love you!

– Eddie Galyean, *Missionary*
Urdaneta City, Pangasinan, Philippines

WE HAD THE wonderful opportunity to have the Boltons with us in Tanzania. They were a great blessing to us and our people. They related very well to our people and have not been forgotten. Mrs. Bolton had the opportunity to teach to our ladies in a ladies meeting. The message that she shared was very touching and enjoyed very much by our ladies. We count the Boltons as dear friends and pray that God will bless their ministry!

– Jerry and Rachel Wyatt, *Missionaries*
Tanzania, Africa

JUST A NOTE to let you know that we are praying for you, don't forget that God probably brought you here to win the previous souls you led to Him on Saturday. I am personally so encouraged by your joyous attitude and spirit. Will never forget your toucan! I taught my kids and husband about the principle you shared with us.

I'm so sorry to hear about your mom. May the Lord comfort you and strengthen you. We love you in the Lord, and you both definitely made an impact on our lives in a way you'll never know!

– Amanda
Church member, "Eden"

I try to read a book a month; however, I read this one in two sittings. I could not put it down! Joanie made me laugh and cry almost simultaneously. The way she expressed her raw emotion when her life was being flipped upside down made her story so relatable. I admire this couple's ministry immensely, and their faith in God and His sovereignty even more. When I grow up I want to be Joanie Bolton!"

~ Jennifer Beil
Former missionary to Ghana

Appendix

THE FOLLOWING LYRICS are from the song "He Is There" by the Hooker family from their CD, "Through the Storm."

When the trials you face turn into darkest night
And you're hoping in some way
The darkness will turn to light,
And you feel all alone,
And no one there with you,
Never fear, my God is holding you.

He is there to comfort you,
When you feel your world is shifting.
He is there to hold you
When everything is changing.
My Lord's still there.

Some days I was so lost,
I just couldn't see Him.
There were moments I felt
My heart would just give in,
But when you're through trying
And there's nothing left to do,
Never fear, my God is holding you.

He is there to comfort you
When you feel your world is shifting.
He is there to hold you
When everything is changing.
My Lord's still there.

He is there (to comfort you)
When you feel your world is shifting.
He is there (to hold you)
When everything is changing.
My Lord's still there.
He is there (He is there)
He is there.

Comforting and Relevant Verses

1 Samuel 12:24

"I will call on the Lord, who is worthy to be praised: so shall I be saved from mine enemies. In my distress I called upon the Lord, and cried to my God: and he did hear my voice out of his temple, and my cry did enter into his ears."

Psalm 26:7

"That I may publish with the voice of thanksgiving, and tell of all thy wondrous works."

Psalm 34:19

"Many are the afflictions of the righteous: but the Lord delivereth him out of them all."

Psalm 37:23

"The steps of a good man are ordered by the Lord: and he delighteth in his way.

Psalm 46:1

"God is our refuge and strength, a very present help in trouble."

Psalm 50:15

"And call upon me in the day of trouble: I will deliver thee, and thou shalt glorify me."

Psalm 55:22

"Cast thy burden upon the LORD, and he shall sustain thee: he shall never suffer the righteous to be moved."

Psalm 56:3

"What time I am afraid, I will trust in thee."

Psalm 57:1

"Be merciful unto me, O God, be merciful unto me: for my soul trusteth in thee: yea, in the shadow of thy wings will I make my refuge, until these calamities be overpast."

Psalm 66:19, 20

"But verily God hath heard me; he hath attended to the voice of my prayer. Blessed be God, which hath not turned away my prayer, nor his mercy from me."

Isaiah 63:7

"I will mention the lovingkindnesses of the LORD, and the praises of the LORD, according to all that the LORD hath bestowed on us...."

Nahum 1:7

"The LORD is good, a strong hold in the day of trouble; and he knoweth them that trust in him."

Matthew 5:4

"Blessed are they that mourn: for they shall be comforted."

Luke 1:74, 75

"That he would grant unto us, that we being delivered out of the hand of our enemies might serve him without fear, In holiness and righteousness before him, all the days of our life.

Romans 8:28

"And we know that all things work together for good to them that love God, to them who are the called according to his purpose."

Romans 8:35, 38-39

"Who shall separate us from the love of Christ? shall tribulation, or distress, or persecution, or famine, or nakedness, or peril, or sword? For I am persuaded, that neither death, nor life, nor angels, nor principalities, nor powers, nor things present, nor things to come, Nor height, nor depth, nor any other creature, shall be able to separate us from the love of God, which is in Christ Jesus our Lord."

Philippians 2:27

"For indeed he was sick nigh unto death: but God had mercy on him; and not on him only, but on me also, lest I should have sorrow upon sorrow."

Hebrews 4:16

"Let us therefore come boldly unto the throne of grace, that we may obtain mercy, and find grace to help in time of need."

James 5:14

"Is any sick among you? let him call for the elders of the church; and let them pray over him, anointing him with oil in the name of the Lord.

Jude 22

"And of some have compassion, making a difference."